Reimagined Plant-Based Indian Recipes

# KARI

Reimagined Plant-Based Indian Recipes

# KARI

**Publisher** Mike Sanders
**Art & Design Director** William Thomas
**Editorial Director** Ann Barton
**Executive Editor** Olivia Peluso
**Assistant Director of Art & Design** Becky Batchelor
**Editorial Assistant** Resham Anand
**Photographer** Sheil Shukla
**Recipe Tester** Bee Berrie
**Copyeditor** West Matuszak
**Proofreaders** Bianca Bosman & Morgan Jefferson
**Indexer** Beverlee Day

First American Edition, 2026
Published in the United States by DK Publishing
1745 Broadway, 20th Floor, New York, NY 10019

The authorized representative in the EEA is Dorling Kindersley Verlag GmbH. Arnulfstr. 124, 80636 Munich, Germany


26 27 28 29 10 9 8 7 6 5 4 3 2 1
001–345441–Aug/2026



A catalog record for this book is available from the Library of Congress.
ISBN 978-0-5939-6171-1



Printed and bound in China

**www.dk.com**

For my little family: Rachel, Shrey, Radhi, and Reva

# CONTENTS



## CORE CURRIES AND HOW TO USE THEM



## CHUTNEYS, DIPS, DRESSINGS, AND MORE!

## HEARTY LEGUMES, GRAINS, AND STEWS



## BREADS



## DRINKS AND DESSERTS



## MENUS

# INTRODUCTION: ON *KARI* AND BELONGING

I've always taken the path less traveled. While I followed a fairly typical premed path, studying molecular biology in college in Chicago, I also studied graphic design—an unconventional pairing that reflected something I've always known: I didn't fit into just one mold. For a long time, not fitting in felt like a burden, but I've since come to see it as a gift. That sense of not belonging gave me permission to explore and follow my curiosity wherever it led.

Growing up, while other kids spent their lunch breaks on the basketball court, I was tucked away in the art studio adding finishing touches to drawings or sculpting clay. I also found community in the school theater, where being different wasn't just accepted—it was the whole point. In college, while peers experimented with house parties and tailgates, I used what I'd learned in my science and art studies to experiment in the kitchen. Instead of relying on dorm food, I taught myself how to cook. And through medical school, I continued to use my kitchen as an extension of my creative identity. I plated meals with intention, treating each dish like a canvas. Food became more than fuel; it was art. It was a quiet rebellion, and ultimately it became a path to belonging as I connected with others with similar passions around me and online. It was during this time that I started sharing my work, combining art and food through my Instagram account and food blog, Plant Based Artist, where I was able to grow a larger community of people interested in food, art, and medicine.

From what I've shared so far, it may surprise you that I grew up in Wisconsin, the land of cheese and beer, but my roots stretch far deeper. My parents emigrated from Ahmedabad, a large city in the northwestern state of Gujarat, India, in the 1970s and settled in a suburb of Milwaukee, where I was born and raised. Our home was a blend of tradition and exploration. At the center of it all was my ba, my paternal grandmother, who lived with us and was the primary cook in our household. She filled our kitchen with the sounds and aromas of mustard seeds and curry leaves frying in hot oil, the rhythm of dough being rolled into thin rotli (whole wheat flatbreads), and the slow bubbling of daal on the stove. Her cooking was rooted in generations of Gujarati culinary wisdom—seasonal, nourishing, and deeply balanced. While we often ate a typical template of rotli, shaak (vegetables), and daal-bhaat (lentils with rice), our family was still very much driven by curiosity. My parents were avid travelers who brought home flavors and stories from across the globe, and Ba was just as open to experimenting and adapting to the world around her. She loved watching cooking shows and browsing grocery stores for ingredients that were new to her, like Dynasty Brown Gravy Sauce, which she'd use to make an incredible broccoli stir fry. She'd substitute zucchini for traditional bottle gourd in her muthiya (spiced dumplings) and always knew when to finish a dish with a pinch of sugar or a squeeze of lime.

*Captions (left to right, top to bottom): 1. My ba (paternal grandmother) and me, 2. My parents and me on a family trip to Alaska, 3. My parents in a suburb of Michigan where they lived prior to settling in Wisconsin, 4. Childhood birthday in Wisconsin, 5. My ba, 6. My mom feeding me as a child at a traditional rite of passage ceremony called janoi, 7. My wife Rachel and me at our Gujarati wedding lunch*

FLAVOR BIBLE

Besharam

INDIA

I later learned, through conversations around the dinner table, that Ba had participated in and won several cooking competitions before she immigrated to the United States. Gujarati by heritage, she had spent her childhood in Kolkata and then moved to Ahmedabad after getting married. Her years in these two large metropolitan areas in India exposed her to cooking traditions from around the country: from east to west and north to south. She brought her rich culinary heritage with her, and that in turn shaped and informed my own culinary background, in a way that's quite similar to many other Asian American and immigrant communities. Ba taught me that food is how we tell stories and build connections. Even though she barely spoke English, she fostered a special friendship with our non-Indian neighbors and even our handyman (who was from Germany), since they loved to garden and always had an abundance of tomatoes, peppers, zucchini, mint, and other produce to share with us. Ba would transform these fresh ingredients into wholesome dishes like her spiced stuffed peppers (bharela marcha) that she'd then share with them.

As much as our family emphasized home cooking, we also enjoyed going out to eat, often at Indian restaurants. North Indian and Punjabi vegetable korma, paneer makhani, saffron rice, naan charred in a tandoor (clay oven)—these dishes were different from what we ate at home. Korma and makhani were incredibly creamy and rich sauces, and the fluffy naan was more indulgent than our humble rotli. They made me realize that even within Indian cuisine there were layers of identity and expression.

That realization expanded even further as I began to explore other Asian cuisines, starting with my family's go-to Thai restaurant, The King and I, which opened in 1988 and is still around today. We craved their panang curry, which was creamy, nutty, spicy, and sweet. It was comforting in the same ways as the Indian restaurant food—and reminded me of my ba's cooking, with deep, balanced flavors. Simultaneously nourishing and nostalgic, curry has become a food I gravitate to.

I've lived most of my adult life in Chicago and the surrounding suburbs. While I've traveled to India many times, my experience with curry and Asian cuisine is largely an American one. It has been shaped by family, restaurants, travel, and community. It's here in the US that I've explored and embraced different interpretations of curry—from Thai gaeng to Japanese karē to Vietnamese cà ri, each with its own unique flavor profile. In Portland, I've been inspired by katsu karē, a rich and mellow curry with just enough sweetness to complement the crispy cutlet. In Washington, DC, I was exposed to the bright and citrusy, lemongrass-forward Vietnamese cà ri. In Chicago, I've enjoyed the deeply aromatic kadala (black chickpea) curry from Thattu, a restaurant highlighting dishes from India's "spice garden," Kerala, on the southern coast.

I now see curry as one of the hallmarks of Asian American cuisine. The word *curry* is derived from the Tamil word *kari* (often associated with spiced dishes or sauces), and over time, it was misapplied by colonizers to describe a vast, diverse set of dishes. And yet, when used thoughtfully, the word *curry* can be a meaningful way to describe a category of food worth celebrating. In this book, I use this word to mean a dish consisting of an aromatic sauce with vegetables and/or proteins, attributed to South Asian and East Asian traditions, often served with rice or bread. Though the ingredients in different types of curries vary, they all evoke similar feelings in the people who eat them: warmth, comfort, balance. It's the common flavors and emotions around curry that I think unify many Asian American communities, and this is the heart of this book.

*Captions (left to right, top to bottom): 1. Rachel and me with chef Margaret and Vinod, owners of Thattu in Chicago, 2. Meal at Thattu, 3. Meal at Besharam in San Francisco, 4. Chef Heena of Besharam and me, 5. Meal at Mirisata in Portland, OR, 6. Meal at Indienne in Chicago*

Whether it's flavored with garam masala, red curry paste, or lemongrass, curry is always comforting and harmonious, and each recipe balances five core flavor profiles: spiced, sweet, sour, salty, and savory. It reflects the layered nature of identity. Home cooks, regardless of background, can easily explore, adapt, and enjoy flavors of other cultures through food. With the help of cookbooks, food media, and friends, I learned to incorporate new and unfamiliar ingredients in my own kitchen. It's these flavors and experiences that have influenced how I cook today and how I use my food to connect with others: from hosting dinner parties to cooking for my family.

The recipes here are rooted in my upbringing as a first-generation Indian American, shaped by the broader flavors of the Asian American diaspora, and driven by a spirit of experimentation. I call it Indo-Asian American cuisine—a way of cooking that honors tradition but isn't confined by it. In the years since I married my wife, Rachel, who is also of Gujarati heritage, we've become avid hosts. We enjoy bringing people together through food: from Diwali parties at our home to kids' birthday parties to smaller get-togethers filled with laughter and conversations on food and art. By cooking up a giant pot of daal for our last Diwali party, we carried forward generations of traditions around food and family. And by preparing and serving dishes inspired by pan-Asian culinary influences like the ones you'll find in this book, we've been able to build community with neighbors, foodies, and artists around us.

This book is ultimately about belonging: through flavor, creativity, and connection. It's about claiming space as someone who never quite fit into a single category. Food is always evolving, and this book reflects that evolution. Today, as a practicing internal medicine physician and a father of three young children, I know how hard it is to get dinner on the table every day. That's why many of the recipes in this book are designed to be flexible, approachable, and practical for everyday life. They're meant to help home cooks build flavor without stress. Chapter one focuses on curries, providing recipes for sauces that can be made ahead and used to build satisfying meals throughout the week. For example, my Tikka Masala Sauce (page 37) can be made on a weekend to enable you to enjoy a restaurant-style Monday dinner without having to order takeout, and any leftover sauce can be used to make bread pizzas (page 41), a kid-friendly meal to help you get past the midweek slump. I also share recipes for similarly versatile sauces and chutneys, like my mango chutney (page 86), which can be served with summery pakoras (page 89) for a dinner party or glazed cauliflower (page 90) for a quick weeknight meal. There are playful desserts and drinks to round out the journey, including cakes I've made for family birthdays for years.

While America is often considered a melting pot, where people of diverse cultures and backgrounds can coexist and thrive, the reality isn't always like that. There's still so much more ground to cover, but if we continue sharing our stories, food memories, and recipes, I am hopeful for a future where we can learn from one another and grow together. This cookbook is my small contribution. Throughout these pages, I credit the voices, dishes, and experiences that have shaped my own—from family recipes to restaurant meals to the beloved cookbooks I've cooked from and learned from along the way. The recipes here are grounded in tradition, infused with creativity, and told through the lens of lived experience. It's a reflection of who I am, the path I've taken, and the way I've used food to explore culture, creativity, health, and connection. More than anything, it's an invitation: to cook, to taste, to experiment, and to make these dishes your own. Whether you grew up with rotli and daal or are discovering these flavors for the first time, I hope this book feels like home. A reminder that there can be unity in diversity. A celebration of food, identity, and all the ways we can belong.

*Photos courtesy of Nimisha Patel Photography*

# A NOTE ON PLANT-BASED EATING

This book reflects how I eat to feel my best, which is plant-based: prioritizing vegetables, fruits, whole grains, legumes, and more. You'll find no meat, fish, dairy, or eggs here. But what you will find are vibrant, satisfying dishes rooted in the flavors and traditions of India, Asia, and beyond—many of which are naturally vegan and others that are thoughtfully adapted with substitutions, like coconut milk or cashew cream in place of dairy and tofu or tempeh in place of animal protein.

During my medical training, I pursued my own nutrition education by attending conferences, connecting with like-minded physicians, and earning a certificate in plant-based nutrition. Through this, I discovered the ways in which food, nutrition, and medicine are interconnected. While I don't believe there is a single perfect diet, I do believe that a diet that prioritizes plants is a way forward. It shouldn't be a surprise that fresh fruits and vegetables, whole grains, legumes, and spices are good for us. These foods are packed with plant protein, fiber, phytonutrients, and antioxidants, and they're the foundation of the recipes in this cookbook. Lentils, chickpeas, tofu, and other legumes are not only versatile and deeply rooted in Asian culinary traditions but are also associated with lower risk of heart disease and even all-cause mortality. Soy (for example, edamame, tofu, and tempeh) in particular contains isoflavones, compounds linked to a lower risk of developing heart disease. And turmeric, long celebrated in Indian kitchens, contains curcumin, which has well-known anti-inflammatory properties. A plant-based diet brings these powerful ingredients to the forefront. Plant-based diets are supported by the Academy of Nutrition and Dietetics, the American College of Lifestyle Medicine, and the American Diabetes Association, just to name a few.

Plant-based eating certainly isn't new. It has many roots in ancient cultures across Asia, which is particularly fitting for this book. In South Asian philosophy, the principle of *ahimsa* (nonviolence) has long influenced vegetarian and plant-forward diets, particularly within Hinduism, Jainism, and Buddhism. That influence can be seen in everyday meals such as the Gujarati thali (which I explore further in my first cookbook, *Plant-Based India*) that celebrate vegetables, legumes, and grains, without any need for animal products.

Still, it's important to acknowledge that dairy and meat hold significant cultural and spiritual meaning in many communities across India and Asia. This book is not meant to erase those traditions but rather to offer an inclusive, modern take on Indian and Asian American cuisine—one that celebrates eating more plant-based foods for our health, for animals, and for the environment.

Many of the foods included in this book, like daal and paratha, are naturally plant-based or require only minimal swaps. Others have been reimagined here: Tofu replaces paneer or chicken in tikka masala, creamy korma is made with beets and hemp seeds instead of dairy or coconut, and salads feature green chutney and tadka. The result is a collection of recipes that feel both familiar and fresh. I hope it serves as a door to deeper exploration, encouraging you to embrace not just the recipes but also your own journey toward nourishment, joy, and feeling your best.

# THE FLAVORS OF *KARI*: SPICED, SWEET, SOUR, SALTY, SAVORY

The recipes in this book seek to achieve harmony among five core flavors—spiced, sweet, sour, salty, and savory (umami). This is a hallmark of many global cuisines, especially Indian and Asian American cooking. The key to mastering this balance at home is simple: Taste as you go. Taste individual ingredients, taste your dish throughout the cooking process, and notice how flavors shift and develop. The more you cook and taste, the more intuitive balancing these flavors will become and the better you'll understand what suits your palate.

## SPICED

Here, *spiced* refers to the depth of flavor that a combination of spices brings to a dish. Spices can be spicy (hot), sweet, cooling, warming, earthy, bitter, or any blend of these flavors. You don't need a pantry full of jars to get started but rather just a handful of versatile, commonly used spices. Many of these can be found in standard grocery stores, while others might require a trip to an Indian or Asian market or an online search.

Consider taking it a step further by supporting brands and small businesses that treat farmers fairly and prioritize equitable sourcing, like Diaspora Spice Co. and Burlap & Barrel. Using spices thoughtfully is one way to honor the people who grow and harvest them.

The spices I use most in my recipes are:

- *Coriander:* citrusy and floral, a requirement in many Indian dishes. I use both coriander seeds and ground coriander. I prefer to grind the seeds in a spice grinder and use within 2 months.
- *Cumin:* slightly woody and earthy, a backbone of Indian cuisine. I call for only whole cumin seeds in this book.
- *Fennel:* provides a nice licorice flavor and sweetness that balances well with other spices like coriander and cumin. I call for only whole fennel seeds in this book.
- *Black mustard seeds:* used in coastal cuisines, including in South Indian, Sri Lankan, and Gujarati dishes. They offer an irreplaceable nuttiness. They can be used interchangeably with brown mustard seeds.
- *Turmeric:* essential in many dishes in this cookbook for both its color and pleasant bitterness when paired with other spices. While whole turmeric root is often used in the preparation of curries, I call for only ground turmeric, since it is easier to keep on hand on a regular basis and is widely available.
- *Peppercorns:* add subtle heat and fruitiness. I use both black and white peppercorns in this book.
- *Chili:* Chilis bring spiciness (heat) to a dish, but they can also provide a fantastic depth, fruitiness, and sometimes smokiness. Generally speaking, for my recipes, you should always add chili to taste. If you know you're sensitive to heat, use less to start and deseed your green chilis. You can always add more heat to a dish, but you can't take it away (though you can add more acid or sugar, or thin with water, if applicable, to tame the heat). A few varieties of chili appear in my recipes:
    - *Indian red chili:* You can find numerous varieties at Indian stores and online, but when I call for ground red chili in this book, I refer to a moderately spicy ground

Indian chili (such as Guntur Sannam chili), slightly coarser than a fine powder. You can substitute other red chili varieties (such as cayenne) to taste.

    - *Green chili:* When I call for green chili, I refer to (from mildest to hottest) jalapeño, green finger chili, serrano, or Thai green chili. Use your favorite variety (I usually use whatever I have on hand) and adjust to your preference.
    - *Paprika:* I call for both smoked and sweet paprika. Smoked paprika is an easy way to add smokiness to a dish (for example, in Tikka Masala Sauce on page 37), while sweet paprika adds a lovely color to the same dish.
    - *Gochugaru:* This is Korean red chili powder, which can vary from fine and powdery to coarse like chili flakes and can also vary in heat level from mild to very hot. I prefer the coarser variety (which is slightly finer than crushed red pepper flakes), mild to moderately spiced. For this, I like Mother-in-Law's brand. Because of the texture (specifically because this version does not have chili seeds) and the nuanced flavor (fruity and subtly smoky), gochugaru is my go-to chili flake in this book. For these recipes, you can substitute Aleppo-style chili flakes or another chili flake variety of your choice.

- *Spice blends:* Spice blends are common in Indian cuisine, and I use a handful of them frequently in the recipes in this book. Here are the spice blends and the brands I used to develop those recipes (you can try other brands, but note that flavors and freshness may vary widely):
    - *Garam masala (Diaspora Spice Co., Tasting India, The Spice House):* a warm blend of toasted spices. Garam masala is often added toward the end of the cooking process for an additional layer of flavor, since it is already bloomed before the spices are ground. Look for spices such as cinnamon, cardamom, cloves, and coriander in the ingredient list.
    - *Curry powder (Burlap & Barrel, S&B, Spicewalla):* a westernized blend of Indian spices that is almost always yellow due to the addition of turmeric. I say "westernized" because in India you'll be hard-pressed to find one single blend of spices that can be used to make any curry; instead, you'll find blends that are specific to certain dishes (such as chana masala, pav bhaji, or biryani). Nonetheless, I do think curry powder as we know it in the West deserves a place in the pantry. It's so versatile, and it's often also used traditionally across Asia. For example, S&B is a Japanese version of curry powder that includes orange, thyme, and sage, which add floral and sweet notes to the blend. Madras curry powder (such as Spicewalla's) can be a touch spicier. For the recipes in this book, use any of these recommended brands.
    - *Five spice (Burlap & Barrel):* a blend of five or more spices (usually star anise, cinnamon, cloves, fennel, and pepper). Five spice is typically sweeter than garam masala. It's used in Chinese and Vietnamese cuisine.
    - *Chai masala (Diaspora Spice Co., Tasting India):* a sweet, floral, and subtly spicy blend of spices used to make chai. It works well in desserts. Look for cardamom, cloves, black pepper, and ginger in the ingredient list.
    - *Chaat masala (Diaspora Spice Co.):* a salty, tangy, umami blend of spices that often includes amchur (dried green mango powder), black salt, and asafetida. I consider this the South Asian take on MSG.

## SWEET

Here are the primary sweeteners you'll see used throughout this book. In savory dishes, feel free to substitute with your preferred sweetener. Just be sure to *taste and adjust* as you go. Sweetness is highly personal, and a little can go a long way.

In the dessert chapter, however, substitutions may require *more careful adjustments and experimentation*, as baking requires more precision and is less forgiving. Wherever possible, I've included notes to guide you.

- *Maple syrup:* I like using maple syrup since I know it traveled the shortest distance to get to me and because it is liquid (so it easily mixes into sauces and stews without needing to dissolve).
- *Palm sugar:* This sugar is caramelly and rich in flavor and derived from the palm tree. It's used most in Thai curries. You can substitute jaggery, a traditional, unrefined South Asian sweetener made from sugarcane juice that has been boiled down. You can also substitute coconut sugar or brown sugar.
- *Cane sugar:* I like to use organic cane sugar, which is still refined but slightly less so than granulated sugar.

## SOUR

Acidity adds brightness and balance to a dish. It cuts through richness and wakes up your palate. You'll find a variety of sour and tangy ingredients used in this book, from citrus juices to vinegars.

In most savory recipes, you can swap one source of acidity for another, depending on what you have on hand and the flavor you're aiming for. Just make sure to *taste as you go.*

- *Citrus:* Lemon and lime provide more fruity and floral notes, while lime also has subtle and pleasant bitter notes.
- *Vinegar:* This is used in various forms throughout the book, including balsamic and distilled white. I like the fruity depth that balsamic vinegar provides in my Garam Masala Balsamic Vinaigrette (page 119) and the neutral acidity that white vinegar provides in my Manchurian Sauce (page 136).
- *Tamarind:* This is called for in a handful of recipes in the book. In addition to offering acidity, tamarind also provides an almost caramelly sweetness and earthiness. I primarily rely on tamarind concentrate, which you can find at Indian grocers. Tamarind concentrate can vary significantly in tartness from brand to brand, so definitely use less to start and add more to taste.

## SALTY

Salt does more than make food taste salty; it *enhances other flavors and makes them shine.* Feel free to adjust the level and source of salt to match your preferences and dietary needs. As always, *season gradually and taste often.* You can always add more, but if you do need to mellow out the salt, you can add more acid or dilute with water if applicable.

- *Salt:* Where I call out salt quantities, I refer to fine sea salt or Himalayan pink salt, since these seemed to be the most popular salts used by my audience when I polled them while I was writing this book. If you prefer Diamond Crystal kosher salt—which many do due to the size of the granules, as it is easier to pinch and more difficult to oversalt—then I suggest doubling the amount of salt called for. That said, please use my salt quantities as a loose guide; it's most important that you get to know your preferred salt and season to taste.
- *Soy sauce:* There are so many different types of soy sauce, but for these recipes, look for a "standard" soy sauce that is labeled neither dark nor light. My go-to brand is San-J.

- *Miso:* There are also so many different types of miso (fermented soy, sometimes also with rice or barley). In these recipes, I use white miso because I like the mellow umami and saltiness that it provides. You can experiment with other types of miso, adjusting to taste as needed. I used Trader Joe's white miso paste when developing the recipes in this book; I like that it has a mellow flavor and dissolves easily into the final sauce or dish.

## SAVORY (UMAMI)

Umami is the elusive "fifth taste." It's what makes dishes taste rich and complete. Ingredients like tomatoes, mushrooms, soy sauce, and even some spices are rich in umami.

Building umami can be as simple as layering ingredients over time or adding just a spoonful of something fermented like miso. Use it to *round out your dish* and make the flavors linger.

- *Miso:* See the note on miso in the Salty section above.
- *Tomato:* I call for canned tomatoes or double concentrated tomato paste (from a tube) in the curries because they're reliable, they don't need to be cooked for a long time, and they're easy to keep throughout the year.
- *Alliums (garlic, onions, shallots, scallions) and ginger:* Alliums are often used in various combinations in many dishes across Asia. I call for both fresh and powdered. Generally, when I call for onions, you can use red, white, or yellow interchangeably. Onions can be used in place of shallots. I often sub in whatever I have on hand. If you need to avoid onions (due to religious or cultural reasons or a dietary intolerance), try experimenting with an equal volume of cabbage or fennel. If you need to avoid garlic for the same reason, simply omit or substitute a pinch of asafetida (described next).
- *Asafetida:* Technically a form of dried and powdered tree sap, this powder offers a savory flavor akin to onions and garlic. Store it in a tightly sealed container; the aroma is pungent and can otherwise take over your pantry. But don't fear—when awoken in hot oil, the aroma mellows and adds nuance.
- *MSG:* See the Headnote on page 136. I don't use this widely in these recipes, but it's nice to have on hand.

# RECIPE AND INGREDIENT NOTES

Before you dig into the recipes to come, here are some additional general recipe and ingredient notes to guide you in achieving the best results.

## TADKA

One of the main South Asian cooking techniques used throughout this book is tadka (Hindi), or tempering (also known by other terms, such as vaghar, in my mother-tongue Gujarati). Tadka is the process of heating oil over medium-high heat and adding whole spices (such as dried chilis, black mustard seeds, cumin seeds, coriander seeds, and fennel seeds), ground spices (such as turmeric, red chili, and asafetida), curry leaves, and/or other aromatics (such as onions, garlic, and ginger). This process fortifies the oil, releasing and awakening natural oils and compounds in the spices and aromatics, which then perfumes a dish. A tadka can be used at the start of preparing a dish (as in many of the curries in this book) or to finish a dish (see Fall Daal, page 161). I've also incorporated the tadka technique in nontraditional ways, as in my Chili Lime Tadka Dressing (page 107) and French Lentils with Lemon Rosemary Tadka (page 162). Use these to think about how you can incorporate tadka in more ways in your own home kitchen. It is nice to have a small saucepan or tadka pan (a small round-bottomed pan with a long handle) reserved for this purpose. Many Indian grocery stores sell tadka pans, or you can find them online.

## TOFU

The three main forms of tofu I call for in this book are silken tofu, extra firm tofu, and super firm (or high protein) tofu. I use soy-based tofu here, but feel free to experiment with tofu varieties made from other legumes (such as Burmese tofu, made from chickpea flour) or seeds (such as pumpkin seed tofu).

- *Silken tofu:* I like the creamy texture that silken tofu provides, and it's used in my Creamy Five Spice Rice Bowl (page 128). Consider blending silken tofu into a curry for added creaminess and plant protein.
- *Extra firm tofu:* When I call for pressing extra firm tofu, you should use a tofu press for best results, but you can also place the tofu between two paper towels or clean kitchen towels. Place a flat plate or cutting board on top of the tofu and a few heavy cans (like beans) or books on top of the plate for up to 60 minutes. Drain the excess water and pat dry with a clean kitchen towel or paper towel when ready to use.
- *Super firm tofu:* Also sold as high protein tofu, this already has as much water pressed out as possible, so it holds up well to the process of making katsu (see page 33).

I'm not particular to any specific brand of tofu, but one of my favorites is Jenny's Organic Extra Firm Tofu, which is made in Chicago from Illinois-grown soybeans. It can be used in recipes that use extra firm or super firm tofu and does not need to be pressed.

## HERBS

I use plenty of fresh herbs, including mint, cilantro, scallions, and lemongrass, that are readily available at grocery stores. I also use curry leaves and fenugreek leaves, which may be more difficult to find outside of Indian grocery stores.

- *Curry leaves:* Fresh curry leaves are used throughout South Asian cuisines, and they offer a wonderful herbaceous and citrusy flavor that's otherwise indescribable. More is more when it comes to curry leaves. If you can't source fresh ones, you can use dry, frozen, or powdered ones, but these all pale in comparison to fresh. That

said, I don't want you to be discouraged if you can't find any version of curry leaves; in most cases, you can just omit them and you'll still end up with a delicious dish!

- *Fenugreek leaves:* Dried fenugreek offers a pleasant bitterness in my Makhani Sauce (page 30) and Tikka Masala Sauce (page 37).

## OILS

The main oil I use in this book is extra virgin olive oil (EVOO), but in instances where I call for neutral oil, this refers to an oil with a more neutral flavor and/or a lower smoke point (such as avocado oil or grapeseed oil). At the end of the day, just experiment with whatever oil you're used to.

*(left to right, top to bottom) Black peppercorns, cumin seeds, coriander seeds, ground Indian red chili, gochugaru, black mustard seeds, ground turmeric, fennel seeds*

# CORE CURRIES AND HOW TO USE THEM

I believe curries deserve the same status and recognition as the esteemed mother sauces of French cuisine. Somewhat unlike the French mother sauces, for which there are many rules, there are many paths to achieving a great curry. Yes, there are commonalities like browning onions or simmering coconut milk, but there's still a wide variation. Not all curries are (or need to be) creamy, but for most of the curries in this chapter, creaminess is a unifying feature. The three primary ingredients I use to achieve this texture are cashews, hemp seeds, and coconut milk. You can also use other nuts (such as blanched almonds or walnuts) as well as silken tofu, nondairy milk or cream, or even sunflower seeds. What I present here are my go-to curries that I make in my own kitchen, taking shortcuts when possible without sacrificing flavor or depth.

# RECIPE MATRIX

If you've been reading until this point, you'll know that I've gone into detail about what curry is and what it means to me (starting on page 11). This chapter leans into the idea of curries as make-ahead sauces, which makes them more weeknight-friendly and accessible to the home cook. I've organized the chapter with a "one sauce, two ways" approach. Recipes are grouped into threes: The first one shows you how to create a curry base, and the two that follow showcase different ways to use the curry sauce. I've included a chart below to provide an overview of the curries you'll find in this chapter and the various ways to use them. I use the terms sauce, curry, and gravy interchangeably in this chapter—use whatever term you prefer!

| SAUCE | Tofu Katsu | Nachos | Tofu Tikka | Bread Pizza | Crispy Potatoes | Uttapam | Silken Tofu and Peas |
|---|---|---|---|---|---|---|---|
| Makhani Sauce | x | x | x | x | x |  | x |
| Tikka Masala Sauce | x | x | x | x | x |  | x |
| Peanut Coconut Curry | x |  | x | x | x | x | x |
| Lemongrass Yellow Curry | x |  | x |  |  | x | x |
| Spinach and Herb Saag | x |  | x | x | x |  | x |
| Beet Korma | x |  | x | x | x |  | x |
| Madras Curry | x |  | x | x | x | x | x |
| Garlicky Cauliflower Puree | x |  | x | x |  |  |  |

| | Noodle Soup | Chickpeas | Panini | Tofu and Cauliflower | Roasted Cauliflower | Seared Mushrooms | Braised Tofu | (Tadka) Pasta |
|---|---|---|---|---|---|---|---|---|
| | | x | x | x | x | x | | x |
| | | x | x | x | x | x | | x |
| | | x | x | x | x | x | | |
| | x | x | | x | x | x | | |
| | | x | x | x | x | x | x | x |
| | | x | x | x | x | x | | x |
| | x | x | x | x | x | x | | |
| | | | x | | | x | x | x |

# MAKHANI SAUCE

Makes 3½ cups (840 ml)

Our sauce journey begins with a classic: makhani, which translates to "buttery" in Hindi and is the foundation of beloved dishes like butter paneer (paneer makhani) and butter chicken (murgh makhani). Recognizable for its mellow orange hue, rich creaminess, and gentle heat, makhani is one of the most iconic North Indian sauces—comforting, crowd-pleasing, and deeply flavorful.

As with many curries, this sauce is all about layering flavors. It starts with what many consider the "holy trinity" of Indian cooking: onions, garlic, and ginger, cooked slowly with a warming mix of spices like coriander, cumin, fennel, and turmeric. Tomato paste adds brightness, depth, and umami, while cashews and garam masala (see page 17) bring a natural sweetness and warmth that round out the sauce's luxurious texture.

Although "makhani" suggests the presence of butter or cream, my version is completely dairy-free, and you won't miss a thing. In fact, many traditional recipes already rely on cashews for creaminess, so I've fully embraced that approach. Simmering the cashews until they're soft and blending them in a high-speed blender gives this makhani its signature silky texture without the dairy. If you need a nut-free option, hemp seeds work beautifully as a substitute.

The spice level is easily adjustable—simply dial the red chili powder up or down. One ingredient I urge you not to skip is dried fenugreek leaves (kasoori methi), which add a subtle, herbaceous bitterness that perfectly complements the sauce's richness. You can find them at most Indian grocers or online.

2 tablespoons olive oil
1 large yellow onion, diced (about 2 cups/300 g)
Salt
1 tablespoon plus 1 teaspoon coriander seeds
2 teaspoons cumin seeds
1 teaspoon fennel seeds
9 garlic cloves, minced (about 3 tablespoons)
1 tablespoon minced ginger
¼ cup (64 g) double concentrated tomato paste
½ teaspoon ground red chili, plus more to taste
½ teaspoon ground turmeric
¾ cup (105 g) unroasted, unsalted cashews
1 tablespoon dried fenugreek leaves
1 teaspoon garam masala

1. Heat the oil in a large pot or Dutch oven over medium heat.
2. Add the onions and ½ teaspoon salt, and cook, stirring frequently with a wooden spoon, until translucent and evenly browned, about 8 minutes. Reduce the heat slightly if needed to prevent the onions from burning.
3. Add the coriander seeds, cumin seeds, and fennel seeds, and stir until fragrant and lightly browned, about 30 seconds.
4. Reduce the heat to medium-low, add the garlic and ginger, and stir until fragrant, about 2 minutes.
5. Add the tomato paste, chili, and turmeric, and stir frequently until deepened in color, about 5 minutes. Add water, 1 to 2 tablespoons at a time, to prevent sticking and burning, if needed.
6. Add the cashews, fenugreek leaves, ½ teaspoon salt, and 3 cups (720 ml) water. Stir to combine and simmer over medium-low heat, stirring regularly to prevent burning, until the mixture is reduced slightly and the cashews start to soften, about 10 minutes. Stir in the garam masala and remove from the heat.
7. Let cool and then transfer to a high-speed blender. Blend until smooth, adding more water as needed. Taste and adjust for salt and heat (chili).
8. Serve as desired or store in an airtight container in the refrigerator for up to 5 days or in the freezer for up to 4 months.

# TOFU KATSU MAKHANI

Serves 4 as a main

This dish is a celebration of textures: crunchy tofu cutlet, creamy Makhani Sauce (page 30), and refreshingly crisp cabbage. It's the epitome of comfort on a plate, regardless of the season. The inspiration is katsu karē, Japanese vegetable curry served with a pork cutlet, and it's easy to see why katsu karē is so beloved—the crispy cutlet and savory gravy together create the perfect bite. Here, that same approach meets Indian flair: We swap the classic Japanese-style curry for North Indian makhani sauce, which has creaminess from the cashews, tang from the tomato, and freshness from the whole spices, including coriander, cumin, and fennel. And, instead of the traditional tonkatsu (pork cutlet), we use tofu. You can also use the katsu breading technique with sliced vegetables like eggplant or sweet potato or even with mushrooms. Or take it further: Turn it into a katsu-makhani sandwich or mix and match the crispy tofu with any curry from this chapter. Once you've mastered the components, the possibilities are endless.

1 cup (125 g) all-purpose flour
1 teaspoon garlic powder
1 teaspoon onion powder
½ teaspoon freshly cracked black pepper
½ teaspoon ground ginger
½ teaspoon ground turmeric
Salt
1 cup (80 g) panko breadcrumbs
One 16-ounce (454 g) block super firm tofu (see Note)
¼ cup (60 ml) neutral oil, plus more as needed, for cooking
½ batch Makhani Sauce (page 30)

### FOR SERVING

Thinly sliced purple cabbage
Thinly sliced scallions
Microgreens, optional

### NOTE

I recommend using super firm tofu, also sold as pressed or high protein tofu, for this recipe. If you can't find super firm tofu, you can press extra firm tofu at home (see page 20).

1. Whisk together the flour, garlic powder, onion powder, black pepper, ginger, and turmeric, and ¾ teaspoon salt in a wide bowl. Whisk together the panko and ¼ teaspoon salt in another wide bowl.
2. Cut the tofu into four slices and pat both sides dry with a clean kitchen towel. One at a time, place each slice into the flour mixture and flip to lightly coat both sides. Transfer to a large tray or plate.
3. Add about ¾ cup (180 ml) water to the remaining flour mixture in a slow stream, whisking to form a thick, pancake-consistency batter.
4. Place one slice of tofu into the batter and flip to lightly coat both sides. Use clean fingers to spread the batter over the tofu and remove any excess. Then, place the tofu into the panko mixture and press the panko evenly onto both sides. Repeat with the remaining three slices and transfer back to the tray or plate.
5. Lay a clean kitchen towel or paper towel (if desired, for easier cleanup) on a sheet pan. Place a wire rack on top and set near the stovetop.
6. Warm about ¼ cup (60 ml) oil (enough to evenly coat the bottom of the skillet) in a large skillet over medium heat. Add the tofu slices and fry until golden brown, about 5 minutes per side. Check occasionally to ensure the coating does not burn. Transfer to the wire rack to cool for about 5 minutes.
7. While the katsu is cooling, warm the Makhani Sauce in a medium saucepan over medium heat. Slice the katsu into strips (about six strips per slab).
8. Divide the Makhani Sauce evenly over four plates, fan out the tofu slices on top, and top with cabbage, scallions, and microgreens, if using. Serve immediately.

# MAKHANI NACHOS

Serves 4 as an appetizer or snack

My wife, Rachel, and I joke that, when game day rolls around, we're really just in it for the snacks—because let's be honest, sometimes the nachos are way more exciting than the actual game. A good plant-based nacho cheese sauce needs to be creamy, tangy, and packed with enough flavor to make you forget there's no actual cheese involved. Enter my Makhani Sauce (page 30), which does all that and makes your chips feel like hall of famers.

This sauce enrobes every chip in a velvety, dreamy blanket of deliciousness—so much so that you might forget you're eating nachos and not some fancy comfort food. Plus, it's the perfect way to use up leftover makhani, though you may find yourself making a batch just for this purpose. So, grab a plate, prepare to get messy, and may the best snack win.

1 tablespoon olive oil
1 teaspoon cumin seeds
3 garlic cloves, minced (about 1 tablespoon)
Pinch of asafetida, optional
One 15-ounce (425 g) can black beans, drained and rinsed
½ batch Makhani Sauce (page 30)
3 to 4 ounces (85 to 113 g) corn tortilla chips
¼ to ½ cup (65 to 130 g) red salsa (your favorite store-bought or homemade)
2 to 3 small red radishes, thinly sliced
Pickled jalapeño slices, to taste
3 to 4 tablespoons fresh cilantro leaves

1. Heat the oil in a medium saucepan over medium heat. Add the cumin seeds and cook until lightly browned and fragrant, a few seconds. Add the garlic and asafetida, if using, and cook until fragrant, 1 to 2 minutes. Add the beans and stir until well combined and heated through, 3 to 5 minutes.
2. Warm the Makhani Sauce in a medium saucepan over medium heat.
3. Evenly spread the tortilla chips onto a large platter. Top with the warmed Makhani Sauce, black beans, salsa, radishes, jalapeños, and cilantro. Serve immediately.

# TIKKA MASALA SAUCE

Makes about 6 cups (1.4 L)

Tikka masala sauce is Makhani Sauce's (page 30) smokier, more tomatoey, and more garlicky cousin. While the origins of this sauce are contentious, most people agree that it was developed by South Asian cooks in Britain. Similar to makhani, it has become popular around the world for its craveable flavors and creamy texture.

I use this sauce most often as the base of my Tofu Tikka Masala (page 38), but it's so versatile that it can work anywhere you'd use a creamy and/or tomato-based sauce: as a pizza sauce (page 41), as a pasta sauce (page 67 and 81), or even thinned down with water to make a soup (served with my Roasted Red Pepper and Giardiniera Panini on page 60). I always find myself making large batches to have on hand.

- 2 tablespoons olive oil
- 1 large red or yellow onion, diced (about 2 cups/300 g)
- Salt
- 2 tablespoons coriander seeds
- 1½ tablespoons cumin seeds
- 1 teaspoon fennel seeds
- 18 garlic cloves, minced (about ¼ cup plus 2 tablespoons/60 g)
- 2 tablespoons minced ginger
- 1 teaspoon ground red chili, plus more to taste
- 1 teaspoon sweet paprika
- ½ teaspoon ground turmeric
- One 14.5-ounce (411 g) can whole peeled tomatoes
- 1 tablespoon double concentrated tomato paste
- ¾ cup (105 g) unroasted, unsalted cashews
- 1 teaspoon garam masala, plus more to taste
- ½ teaspoon smoked paprika, optional
- 3 tablespoons dried fenugreek leaves (see Headnote on page 30)

1. Heat the oil in a large pot or Dutch oven over medium heat.
2. Add the onions and ½ teaspoon salt, and cook, stirring frequently with a wooden spoon, until translucent and evenly browned, about 8 minutes. Reduce the heat slightly if needed to prevent the onions from burning.
3. Add the coriander seeds, cumin seeds, and fennel seeds, and stir until fragrant and lightly browned, about 30 seconds.
4. Reduce the heat to medium-low, add the garlic and ginger, and stir until fragrant, about 2 minutes. Add the chili, paprika, and turmeric, and stir until well combined, a few seconds.
5. Add the tomatoes and tomato paste, increase the heat slightly, and continue to cook until thickened and deep red in color, about 8 minutes.
6. Add the cashews, 4 cups (960 ml) water, and ½ teaspoon salt, and simmer over medium-low heat, partly covered, until the mixture starts to thicken and the cashews soften, about 15 minutes.
7. Remove from the heat and stir in the garam masala and smoked paprika, if using.
8. Allow the sauce to cool (remove it from the pan and add a few ice cubes to speed up the process). Transfer to a high-speed blender, add 1½ cups (360 ml) water, and blend until very smooth.
9. Taste and adjust for salt, warmth (garam masala), and heat (chili). Crush the fenugreek leaves between your fingers and stir into the blended sauce.
10. Serve as desired or store in an airtight container in the refrigerator for up to 5 days or in the freezer for up to 4 months.

# TOFU TIKKA MASALA

Serves 4 as a main

For my wife, Rachel, and me, this dish is pure nostalgia in a pot. Growing up in households centered around simple, homestyle Gujarati cuisine, we didn't get to experience the magic of tikka masala at home. That's largely because this dish often requires the use of a tandoor (clay oven), which is very much not commonplace in Indian home kitchens due to its large size and very high temperatures (and the skill it takes to use it). So, we both sought out tikka masala at local Indian restaurants—hers in Illinois, mine in Wisconsin—where it became a beloved favorite. It took me years to develop a dairy-free version that truly honors those cherished memories. The secret? Nearly two whole bulbs of garlic per batch, which infuse the sauce with unforgettable depth.

Tikka masala is often prepared with paneer or chicken that has been marinated in aromatics and spices and roasted in a tandoor. Tofu is a natural plant-based stand-in for the traditional proteins. To capture the subtle smokiness found in restaurant versions, I recommend browning the tofu in a skillet and adding a touch of smoked paprika. You can also broil the tofu for extra char, but skillet cooking offers more control and reduces the risk of burning. Feel free to adjust the smoked paprika to your taste—or skip it altogether. Other protein options like seitan or tempeh work wonderfully as well.

One 16-ounce (454 g) block super firm tofu (see Note)
2 tablespoons olive oil, divided
3 garlic cloves, minced (about 1 tablespoon)
1 tablespoon lemon juice (from about ½ lemon)
1 teaspoon ground coriander
1 teaspoon garam masala
1 teaspoon grated ginger
1 teaspoon onion powder
1 teaspoon sweet paprika
½ teaspoon ground red chili
½ teaspoon cumin seeds
½ teaspoon ground turmeric
½ teaspoon smoked paprika, optional
Salt
1 batch Tikka Masala Sauce (page 37)

### FOR SERVING

2 tablespoons chopped fresh cilantro leaves or microgreens, optional
Fluffy Basmati Rice (page 154) or Garlic Naan (page 178)

1. Tear or cut the tofu into bite-size pieces and place in a large bowl.
2. Combine 1 tablespoon oil and the garlic, lemon juice, coriander, garam masala, ginger, onion powder, sweet paprika, chili, cumin seeds, turmeric, and smoked paprika, if using, and ½ teaspoon salt in a small bowl. Stir to form a paste and then transfer to the large bowl with the tofu. Stir to coat the tofu pieces evenly.
3. Heat the remaining 1 tablespoon oil in a large oven-safe nonstick or cast-iron skillet over medium-high heat. Add the tofu and sear until browned, about 5 minutes. Stir and cook until browned on most sides, 5 to 10 minutes. Place under the broiler or use a blowtorch to char the pieces, if desired. Taste and adjust for salt.
4. Warm the Tikka Masala Sauce in a medium saucepan over medium heat. Add the cooked tofu, top with cilantro, if using, and serve immediately with rice or naan.

### NOTE

I recommend using super firm tofu, also sold as pressed or high protein tofu, for this recipe. If you can't find super firm tofu, you can press extra firm tofu at home (see page 20).

# TIKKA MASALA BREAD PIZZA

Makes 4 pizzas

Bread pizza—a slice of bread topped with sauce, cheese, and veggies—was a go-to meal for me in college and medical school. Quick, easy, comforting, and satiating, this recipe is a great way to use up even small quantities of leftover Tikka Masala Sauce (page 37). With this technique, you can use up any of the sauces in this chapter for a quick and satisfying meal or snack. And don't limit yourself to the bell peppers and onions I use here: Chopped broccoli, zucchini, olives, mushrooms, and spinach are also great veggie toppings. I have one rule: Have fun with it!

4 slices sourdough bread (from an 8-inch/20 cm loaf)
¾ cup (180 ml) Tikka Masala Sauce (page 37)
1 cup (90 g) mozzarella-style vegan cheese
1 small bell pepper, diced
1 small red onion, diced
1½ teaspoons dried herb blend (such as Italian seasoning, pizza seasoning, or herbes de Provence)
Freshly cracked black pepper, to taste
Drizzle of olive oil, optional

1. Preheat the oven to 425°F (220°C). Place the bread slices on a sheet pan in a single layer.
2. Spread about 3 tablespoons Tikka Masala Sauce onto each slice of bread in an even, thin layer.
3. Evenly distribute the cheese, bell peppers, onions, and herbs onto each slice. Top with black pepper and a drizzle of oil, if using.
4. Bake for 15 minutes, until the cheese is fully melted and starting to brown. For more browning, place the pan under the broiler for about 1 minute, watching carefully to prevent burning.
5. Cut into slices and serve immediately.

# PEANUT COCONUT CURRY

Makes 2 cups (480 ml)

This curry is a vibrant meeting point between Indian and Thai cuisines, inspired by my favorite comforting Thai curries: panang and Massaman. Panang is a creamy coconut-based curry with a nuttiness that comes from ground peanuts. Massaman incorporates spices like cinnamon, clove, cumin, and coriander, which are also staples in Indian cuisine, and contains whole peanuts.

I leaned into these shared elements in this curry, through coconut milk, Thai red curry paste, peanut butter, and garam masala, and added more of an Indian touch with mustard seeds and curry leaves, nodding to both Gujarati and South Indian cooking. These ingredients pair beautifully with the peanutty coconut base and echo the flavors of Gujarati daal and South Indian peanut and coconut chutneys.

The result is a shining example of the spicy (red curry paste), sweet (palm sugar), sour (tamarind), salty (miso), and savory (peanut butter and miso) flavor balance that is a hallmark of great curries. Use this recipe as a starting point, tasting it as you go, and you'll soon enough be on your way to achieving your own perfect version of this rich, cross-cultural curry. The star anise, while optional, provides a sweetness and subtle smokiness.

One 13.5-ounce (400 ml) can coconut milk (see Note 1), divided
10 to 12 fresh curry leaves, thinly sliced
½ teaspoon cumin seeds
½ teaspoon black mustard seeds
3 tablespoons Thai red curry paste (see Note 2)
¼ teaspoon ground turmeric
¼ cup (65 g) smooth peanut butter
2 tablespoons palm sugar or light brown sugar
1 tablespoon white miso
1 star anise, optional
1 teaspoon garam masala
½ to 1 teaspoon tamarind concentrate or lime juice, to taste

1. Heat about ¼ cup (60 ml) coconut milk in a large saucepan over medium-high heat, stirring frequently, until it thickens and the oil starts to separate, about 3 minutes.
2. Add the curry leaves, cumin seeds, and mustard seeds, and stir until the mustard seeds start to pop, about 30 seconds.
3. Add the curry paste and turmeric, and stir frequently until the mixture becomes very fragrant and the oil starts to separate, about 5 minutes.
4. Add the remaining coconut milk and the peanut butter, sugar, miso, star anise (if using), and 1 cup (240 ml) water. Stir well and simmer over low heat, stirring occasionally, until thickened, 10 to 15 minutes.
5. Stir in the garam masala and tamarind and then remove from the heat. Remove star anise just before serving (if using).
6. Serve as desired or store in an airtight container in the refrigerator for up to 5 days or in the freezer for up to 4 months.

NOTES

1 Used in a few of the curry recipes, coconut milk (canned) offers a nice creamy consistency that is characteristic of Thai, South Indian, Sri Lankan, and Vietnamese curries. When coconut milk is cooked, the oil can separate, resulting in a layer of oil atop the curry. The oil separation is actually an often-desired characteristic of Thai curries. If this does not appeal to you, drain with caution (the oil will have a ton of flavor that you'll otherwise miss out on). Sometimes adding peanut butter (as I do here) can help emulsify the curry.

2 Thai curry paste can be spicy, and different brands are not created equal, so if you are sensitive to heat, I recommend reducing the quantity of curry paste to 1 to 2 tablespoons. But if you love heat, you can easily increase it to 4 to 6 tablespoons. I use Maesri red curry paste, which is widely available at Asian grocery stores and online.

# CRISPY POTATOES

## *with Peanut Coconut Curry*

Serves 4 as a side

Potatoes and peanuts are classic additions to Massaman curry, which inspired the Peanut Coconut Curry (page 42) I've paired them with here. While Massaman features creamy and tender potatoes that almost melt in the curry, this dish takes a slight pivot and celebrates texture contrast—crispy smashed potatoes, crunchy crushed peanuts, and creamy curry sauce. This dish is intended to be an appetizer or side, but you can add in other vegetables (such as broccoli and carrots) and protein (such as tofu or chickpeas) and serve with rice to make a more complete meal.

1½ pounds (680 g) baby potatoes, scrubbed
Salt
2 to 3 tablespoons olive oil
Freshly cracked black pepper
1 batch Peanut Coconut Curry (page 42)
¼ cup (36 g) roasted peanuts, chopped

**FOR SERVING**

2 to 3 scallions, sliced
2 to 3 tablespoons roughly chopped fresh cilantro leaves

1. Preheat the oven to 425°F (220°C). Line a sheet pan with parchment paper.
2. Place the potatoes in a large pot with enough water to submerge them. Add about 1 tablespoon salt and bring to a boil over medium-high heat. Boil until fork tender, 10 to 15 minutes, depending on the size of your potatoes.
3. Drain the potatoes and then dry them with a clean kitchen towel. Transfer to the sheet pan and smash one potato at a time with the bottom of a glass or bowl.
4. Drizzle the potatoes with the oil until evenly coated.
5. Roast for 15 minutes, or until starting to brown. Remove from the oven, flip the potatoes over, and roast for 15 minutes, or until browned and crispy on the edges. Season with salt and black pepper to taste.
6. To serve, warm the Peanut Coconut Curry in a medium saucepan over medium heat and then place on a large serving dish. Top with the potatoes, peanuts, scallions, and cilantro, and serve immediately.

# UTTAPAM

## *with Peanut Coconut Curry*

Makes 10 to 15 uttapam

Uttapam is a savory South Indian "pancake" made from a batter of fermented rice and urad daal and topped with vegetables. It's traditionally served for breakfast, but I think it makes for a great meal at any time of day. I like to add quinoa to my batter because it provides extra nuttiness, fiber, and protein, but you can omit it and add an equal amount of rice for a more traditional version. This recipe requires you to make the batter the day before, but I promise it's well worth the wait. The batter also keeps well in the fridge (see Tip 1), so you can make it over the weekend for a quick and easy weeknight dinner. While I serve it with my Peanut Coconut Curry (page 42) here, you can also serve it with Madras Curry (page 70), Green Chutney Tahini Sauce (page 98), or even ketchup.

These uttapam are made with just bell peppers and onions, but you can certainly add other vegetables and toppings, such as finely diced or grated carrots, scallions, diced tomatoes, or green chilis. In the summer, I even like adding nasturtium leaves and flowers or squash blossoms when they're in season.

### BATTER

1 cup (200 g) white urad daal (also known as urad gota) or split white urad daal
1 cup (190 g) quinoa
½ cup (100 g) medium-grain white rice (such as sona masuri)
½ teaspoon fenugreek seeds
Salt

### UTTAPAM

1 batch Peanut Coconut Curry (page 42)
Neutral oil, for cooking
1 large red onion, diced (about 2 cups/300 g)
2 to 3 small bell peppers, diced (about 2 cups/200 g)
3 to 4 tablespoons chopped fresh cilantro leaves, optional

1. Make the batter: Rinse the urad daal, quinoa, rice, and fenugreek seeds together in a fine-mesh strainer, agitating with your fingers, until the water runs mostly clear. Transfer to a large bowl and add plenty of room-temperature water to cover by at least a few inches. Cover with a plate or lid and set aside at room temperature to soak for 3 to 4 hours or up to 12 hours.
2. Drain and add to a blender along with 1½ cups (360 ml) water. Blend until mostly smooth; the mixture should resemble wet sand. Transfer to a large bowl (at least triple the size of the batter), cover with a plate or lid, and place in a warm spot (such as in the oven with the oven light on) to ferment for 10 to 12 hours. You'll know it's ready if it looks fluffy when you scoop into the batter with a spoon or ladle. If it does not, you can ferment for longer, ensuring the environment is not too cool. Stir in 1 teaspoon salt (or more to taste, after cooking the first uttapam) and set aside. If making the batter ahead of time, transfer to the refrigerator (see Tip 1).
3. Just prior to making the uttapam, warm the Peanut Coconut Curry in a medium saucepan over medium heat.
4. Make the uttapam: Heat a medium nonstick or cast-iron skillet over medium-high heat. Brush a thin layer of oil onto the skillet and then ladle in ⅓ to ½ cup (80 to 120 ml) batter in a thin layer (about ¼ inch/6 mm). Reduce the heat to medium and sprinkle on an even layer of onions, bell peppers, and cilantro, if using. Drizzle about 1 teaspoon oil around the edges of the uttapam.
5. Cook until bubbles start to form on top of the uttapam and/or the bottom starts to brown, about 3 minutes. Flip and continue to cook until browned on the other side, 2 to 3 minutes. Transfer the cooked uttapam to a large plate and cover with a bowl or foil to keep warm.
6. Repeat steps 4 and 5 to make and cook the remaining uttapam (see Tip 2). Serve with the warmed curry as a dipping sauce.

**TIPS**

1 If making the batter ahead of time, store it in an airtight container (after fermenting) in the refrigerator for up to 5 days. When ready to use, leave at room temperature for 1 to 2 hours prior to cooking and add salt just prior to using.

2 While it's easier to make all of the uttapam at once and then serve, I recommend eating them right off the stovetop; they will have a slight crispiness that is incredibly satisfying.

*Uttapam with scallions, nasturtium leaves, and flowers*

# LEMONGRASS YELLOW CURRY

Makes 2 cups (480 ml)

The bright, sweet, and citrusy fragrance of lemongrass is a hallmark of many Vietnamese dishes, especially Vietnamese-style curry (cà ri), a coconut-based curry infused with curry powder and lemongrass. I wanted to capture that scent in this curry, which also draws influence from many coconut-based Sri Lankan curries that contain lemongrass, lime leaves, and/or curry leaves. This recipe uses curry leaves, which are citrusy and earthy, or lime leaves, which are citrusy and sweet. Both versions are equally delicious. If you can't find fresh leaves, look for dry or frozen, and omit them only if you must. Be sure to keep the leaves and lemongrass nestled in the curry for as long as possible to get the most flavor out of them. It's even better to leave this curry in the fridge overnight before enjoying; this really ties together all the flavors.

- One 13.5-ounce (400 ml) can coconut milk, divided
- 4 to 6 fresh curry leaves or makrut lime leaves, torn
- ½ teaspoon black mustard seeds
- ¼ teaspoon fenugreek seeds, optional
- 2 to 3 shallots or 1 small onion, finely diced (about 1 cup/150 g)
- Salt
- 5 garlic cloves, minced (about 1½ tablespoons)
- 1 jalapeño (or preferred green chili), seeded for milder spice, minced
- 1 lemongrass stalk, cut into 2-to-3-inch (5 to 7.5 cm) chunks and smashed with the dull side of a knife
- 1 tablespoon minced ginger
- ½ teaspoon ground turmeric
- Freshly cracked black pepper, to taste
- 1 tablespoon palm sugar or preferred sweetener
- 1 to 2 teaspoons lime juice (from about ½ lime)

1. Heat about ¼ cup (60 ml) coconut milk in a large saucepan over medium heat, stirring frequently, until it thickens and the oil starts to separate, about 3 minutes.
2. Add the curry leaves, mustard seeds, and fenugreek seeds, if using, and stir until the mustard seeds start to pop, about 30 seconds.
3. Add the shallots and ½ teaspoon salt, reduce the heat to medium-low, and stir frequently until the shallots become translucent and start to brown, about 5 minutes.
4. Add the garlic, jalapeño, lemongrass, ginger, turmeric, and black pepper, and stir until fragrant, about 1 minute.
5. Add the remaining coconut milk, the sugar, 1 cup (240 ml) water, and ¼ teaspoon salt, and simmer, stirring occasionally, until the sugar dissolves and the curry thickens to your desired consistency, 10 to 15 minutes.
6. Remove from the heat, stir in lime juice to taste, and adjust salt to taste. Remove the curry leaves and lemongrass just prior to serving. Serve as desired or store in an airtight container in the refrigerator for up to 5 days or in the freezer for up to 4 months.

# LEMONGRASS YELLOW CURRY

## *with Silken Tofu and Peas*

Serves 2 to 4 as a main

While it's not a traditional combination, something magical happens when you combine silken tofu with an aromatic, creamy curry. Here, the tofu sops up the luscious citrusy and vibrant yellow coconut curry, and the peas offer a welcome pop of color and texture. Since I photograph all of my recipes, my family knows all too well that the camera needs to eat first in our house when I'm developing recipes. As a result, I happily discovered that this dish works just as well warm as it does chilled or at room temperature.

One 16-ounce (454 g) container silken tofu, drained
1 cup (130 g) frozen or fresh peas
1 batch Lemongrass Yellow Curry (page 51)

**FOR SERVING, OPTIONAL**

2 scallions, thinly sliced, or 2 tablespoons roughly chopped fresh cilantro leaves
Fluffy Basmati Rice (page 154)

1. Scoop the tofu into a serving bowl.
2. Bring a large saucepan of water to a boil. Add the peas and cook until tender, 3 to 5 minutes. Strain and add the peas to the tofu bowl.
3. Warm the Lemongrass Yellow Curry in the same saucepan over medium heat and pour it over the tofu and peas. Top with scallions or cilantro, if using. Serve on its own or with rice.

# LEMONGRASS YELLOW CURRY NOODLE SOUP

## *with Tempeh*

Serves 2 to 3 as a main

I'll admit that I was never a fan of tempeh due to its bitterness and grainy texture. But I like a challenge, and I was determined to make a version that I could enjoy, since tempeh is a great source of protein and fiber. And since it's difficult not to like the slurpy goodness of a noodle soup, I figured adding tempeh to one would be a good starting point. The sweetness from hoisin sauce and five spice powder balances out the bitter nuttiness of the tempeh, and this is what finally made me a tempeh lover. By crumbling the tempeh, you create a greater surface area for absorbing flavor. So, whether you like tempeh or not, give this a try. Don't skimp on using a variety of fresh herbs to top it all off; this provides a refreshing brightness to every bite.

### TEMPEH

1 tablespoon neutral oil
3 garlic cloves, minced (about 1 tablespoon)
2 scallions, minced
½ tablespoon minced ginger
8 ounces (227 g) crumbled tempeh
2 tablespoons hoisin sauce
1 teaspoon rice vinegar
1 teaspoon soy sauce
1 teaspoon sriracha
½ teaspoon five spice powder

### NOODLE SOUP

4 ounces (113 g) dry rice vermicelli noodles
1 medium head broccoli, cut into bite-size florets
1 batch Lemongrass Yellow Curry (page 51)

### FOR SERVING

¼ cup (5 to 10 g) chopped fresh herbs (such as mint, cilantro, basil, or, ideally, a combination)
2 to 3 scallions, thinly sliced
Thinly sliced chilis (such as Fresno or jalapeño), to taste, optional
Lime wedges, optional

1. Make the tempeh: Heat the oil in a large nonstick pan over medium heat. Add the garlic, scallions, and ginger, and heat until fragrant and softened, about 3 minutes. Add the tempeh and stir frequently until it starts to brown, about 5 minutes.
2. Add the hoisin sauce, rice vinegar, soy sauce, sriracha, and five spice powder, and stir until well combined. Continue to cook until the tempeh is sticky and the sauce begins to caramelize, about 5 minutes. Remove from the heat.
3. Make the noodle soup: Bring a large saucepan of water to a boil. Boil the rice noodles until tender, 2 to 5 minutes. Use tongs to remove the noodles and divide them evenly between two or three serving bowls. In the same pot of boiling water, cook the broccoli until bright green and fork tender, 2 to 3 minutes. Drain and divide evenly between the serving bowls.
4. Warm the Lemongrass Yellow Curry in a medium saucepan over medium heat, adding a few tablespoons of water, if needed, to maintain a soupy consistency. Divide evenly between the serving bowls. Top with the tempeh, fresh herbs, scallions, and chili slices, if using. Squeeze lime wedges on top, if desired, and serve immediately.

# SPINACH AND HERB SAAG

Makes 3½ cups (840 ml)

Saag, a North Indian gravy made from greens (most commonly mustard greens or spinach), is one of my favorite ways to use up any leftover greens in my fridge. This version highlights spinach as the main green, though you can use baby kale or stemmed green kale, with cilantro or mint for more vibrancy and herbaceous notes. You can easily sub more mint for cilantro if you're not a cilantro lover—no fear! I also add miso here for added umami and to mellow out the bitterness from the greens.

2 tablespoons olive oil
1 large yellow onion, diced (about 2 cups/300 g)
Salt
1 tablespoon coriander seeds
2 teaspoons cumin seeds
1 teaspoon fennel seeds
12 garlic cloves, minced (about ¼ cup/45 g)
1 jalapeño (or preferred green chili), seeded for milder spice, minced
1 tablespoon minced ginger
5 ounces (142 g) baby spinach
½ cup (about 30 g) packed fresh cilantro leaves and stems
½ cup (about 14 g) packed fresh mint leaves
1 cup (240 g) ice (see Note)
2 tablespoons white miso, or more to taste
2 teaspoons lime juice (from about ½ lime), plus more to taste
½ teaspoon garam masala

1. Heat the oil in a large pot over medium heat.
2. Add the onions and ½ teaspoon salt, and cook, stirring frequently with a wooden spoon, until translucent and evenly browned, about 8 minutes. Reduce the heat slightly if needed to prevent the onions from burning.
3. Add the coriander seeds, cumin seeds, and fennel seeds, and stir until fragrant and lightly browned, about 30 seconds.
4. Reduce the heat to medium-low, add the garlic, jalapeño, and ginger, and stir until fragrant and starting to brown, about 2 minutes.
5. Add 1 cup (240 ml) water and bring to a gentle simmer. Add the spinach, cilantro, and mint, and cook until just wilted, 2 to 3 minutes.
6. Remove from the heat and transfer to a large bowl. Stir in the ice, miso, lime juice, and garam masala, and let cool for a few minutes. Transfer to a blender and blend until smooth. Taste and adjust for salt and acid (lime juice).
7. Serve as desired or store in an airtight container in the refrigerator for up to 3 days. This is best served fresh.

**NOTE**
The ice, while not traditionally essential to making saag, is used here to quickly cool down the mixture, which helps retain the vibrant green color of the greens and makes it easier on your blender to blend right away.

# CHANA SAAG

Serves 2 to 4

Because chickpeas (chana in Hindi) are a good blank canvas for flavor, they work particularly well with saag (and pretty much any other curry in this chapter). This is a classic combination, often appearing on Indian restaurant menus as chana saag or saag chhole. I like to wake up chickpeas from a can by sautéing them with cumin and turmeric, but if you're able to plan ahead, I encourage you to cook your chickpeas from dry. The chickpeas become tender and buttery and almost melt into the sauce (see Note).

1 tablespoon olive oil
½ teaspoon cumin seeds
One 16-ounce (454 g) can chickpeas, drained and rinsed
¼ teaspoon ground turmeric
Salt
½ batch Spinach and Herb Saag (page 56)

**FOR SERVING**

Gochugaru or crushed red pepper flakes, optional
Fluffy Basmati Rice (page 154), naan (page 178), flatbread, or toasted sourdough

1. Heat the oil in a large pan over medium heat.
2. Add the cumin seeds and cook until fragrant and starting to brown, 1 to 2 minutes.
3. Add the chickpeas, turmeric, and ¼ teaspoon salt, and stir until the chickpeas are heated through and starting to brown, 3 to 5 minutes.
4. Warm the Spinach and Herb Saag in a medium saucepan over medium heat, transfer to a serving bowl, if desired, and top with the chickpeas. Garnish with gochugaru, if using, and serve with rice or bread.

**NOTE**

To make enough chickpeas for about two batches of this recipe, soak 1 cup (200 g) dry chickpeas in cool water overnight. Drain and then transfer to a large pot filled with several inches of water. Add a halved shallot or onion, a few garlic cloves, and a bay leaf. Bring to a boil and reduce the heat to medium-low to maintain a gentle simmer for about 1 hour, or until the chickpeas are tender. Add a pinch of baking soda if you prefer a creamy and tender chickpea, like I do. Add salt to taste in the last 10 minutes of cooking. If you cook your chickpeas at home, skip the sauté step and add them directly to the saag or other curry of choice.

# ROASTED RED PEPPER AND GIARDINIERA PANINI

*with Saag*

Serves 1

I'm of the school of thought that any grilled sandwich is infinitely better when dunked into a thick stew or soup. My Spinach and Herb Saag (page 56) serves that role here; the toasted bread from the panini soaks up the saag and balances perfectly with the cheesy and spicy interior. I add Chicago-style giardiniera—Italian spicy pickled peppers and vegetables such as carrots and cauliflower—as a tribute to Chicagoland, where I've been living all of my adult life. Chicago-style giardiniera differs from others in that the vegetables are more finely chopped like a relish, and it is packed in oil instead of brine. If you're not able to find Chicago-style giardiniera, you can easily substitute other varieties of giardiniera or even pickled jalapeños. While it's nice to have a panini press for this recipe, you certainly don't need one (see Tip).

2 slices sourdough bread (from an 8-inch/20 cm loaf)
2 slices mozzarella-style vegan cheese (or 2 to 3 tablespoons Lemony Coriander and Fennel Tofu "Ricotta," page 131)
2 tablespoons chopped roasted red peppers
1 tablespoon mild or hot Chicago-style giardiniera, excess oil drained and finely chopped
Freshly cracked black pepper, to taste
½ cup (120 ml) Spinach and Herb Saag (page 56)
1 to 2 teaspoons olive oil

1. Preheat an electric panini press to medium-high heat.
2. Place one slice of bread on a plate and add the cheese in an even layer. Add the red peppers, giardiniera, and black pepper. Top with the other slice of bread.
3. Warm the Spinach and Herb Saag in a medium saucepan over medium heat.
4. While the saag is warming, brush the sandwich with oil on both sides and cook in the panini press until grill marks form. Remove from the press, cut in half, and serve with the warmed saag as a dip.

**TIP**

If you don't have a panini press, assemble the sandwich and then heat a grill pan or skillet over medium heat. Cook the sandwich until browned and crisp on both sides, about 5 minutes per side.

# BEET KORMA

Makes 2½ cups (600 ml)

Korma is a sometimes-mellow, often-luxurious curry rooted in the royal Mughlai cuisine of South Asia, made with nuts, dairy, and/or coconut milk for creaminess. In this version, I've omitted all of those ingredients to make an allergen-friendly version that makes use of hemp seeds with no sacrifice of flavor or texture.

My inspiration for including beets in this korma is partly seasonal—when I was growing up in the Midwest, beets were a fall staple, often roasted or served in salads. This recipe is a nod to that regional familiarity, blended with the structure and flavor profile of a korma. While beets aren't commonly used in kormas, they are used in traditional dishes such as poriyal, a South Indian stir fry with coconut and mustard seeds, or raita, a North Indian yogurt condiment. Here, they offer a bridge between traditions and an incredibly vibrant color. The beets and the hemp seeds give this korma a pleasant earthiness perfect for fall in the Midwest (or anywhere else, for that matter).

Use the building blocks here to modify to your heart's desire: Try using almonds or other nuts instead of the hemp seeds for creaminess or another starchy vegetable, such as carrots or butternut squash, in place of the beets.

2 tablespoons olive oil
1 large white or yellow onion, diced (about 2 cups/300 g)
2 to 3 small beets, peeled and diced (about 1 cup/140 g)
Salt
2 teaspoons coriander seeds
2 teaspoons cumin seeds
6 garlic cloves, minced (about 2 tablespoons)
1 tablespoon minced ginger
½ teaspoon ground red chili, plus more to taste
½ teaspoon ground turmeric
½ cup (70 g) hemp seeds
1 teaspoon garam masala

1. Heat the oil in a large pot over medium heat. Add the onions, beets, and ½ teaspoon salt, and cook, stirring frequently with a wooden spoon, until the onions are translucent, the beets have softened, and both are starting to brown, 10 to 15 minutes.
2. Add the coriander seeds and cumin seeds, and stir until fragrant and lightly browned, about 30 seconds.
3. Reduce the heat to medium-low. Add the garlic, ginger, chili, and turmeric, and stir until fragrant, about 2 minutes.
4. Add the hemp seeds and 1 cup (240 ml) water, and bring to a gentle simmer. Simmer until the beets are very soft and can be easily mashed with a fork and most of the water has evaporated, 5 to 10 minutes. Stir in the garam masala and remove from the heat.
5. Let cool slightly and then transfer to a blender. Blend until smooth, adding ½ to ¾ cup (120 to 180 ml) water to achieve a saucy consistency. Taste and adjust for salt and heat (chili).
6. Serve as desired or store in an airtight container in the refrigerator for up to 3 days. This is best served fresh.

# BEET KORMA
## *with Tofu and Cauliflower*

Serves 2 to 4 as a main

I absolutely love pairing cauliflower and tofu in a curry—both are fantastic at soaking up bold flavors, making every bite rich and comforting. Cauliflower brings a toothsome texture and subtle sweetness, while tofu provides a hearty protein boost, creating a perfectly balanced meal that's both nourishing and delicious. In this recipe, I roast the cauliflower to caramelize it and bring out its natural nuttiness, and I pan-fry the tofu to achieve a crispy, golden exterior that contrasts beautifully with the creamy curry. You can apply this method of roasting cauliflower and pan-frying tofu with almost any curry in this chapter, turning your favorite sauces into complete, well-rounded meals.

1 medium head cauliflower, cut into florets
2 to 3 tablespoons olive oil, divided
Salt
One 16-ounce (454 g) block super firm tofu (see Note), cut into two-bite triangles
1 teaspoon ground turmeric, divided
1 batch Beet Korma (page 63)
Hemp seeds, for garnish, optional
Fluffy Basmati Rice (page 154), naan (page 178), any flatbread, or toasted sourdough, for serving

1. Preheat the oven to 425°F (220°C). Line 2 sheet pans with parchment paper (if desired, for easier cleanup).
2. Place the cauliflower in a single layer on the sheet pans. Drizzle 1 to 2 tablespoons oil onto the cauliflower and sprinkle with salt to taste. Massage the oil into the cauliflower pieces and roast for 15 to 20 minutes, until tender and browned on the edges.
3. While the cauliflower is roasting, prepare the tofu. Heat 1 tablespoon oil in a large nonstick pan over medium heat. Add the tofu in a single layer and sprinkle with about ½ teaspoon turmeric and salt to taste.
4. Cook until the tofu starts to brown, about 5 minutes. Then flip, sprinkle with the remaining ½ teaspoon turmeric and more salt, and cook until browned on the other side, about 5 minutes. Flip the pieces over again, and swirl in the pan to evenly spread the turmeric, 1 to 2 minutes. Remove from the heat.
5. Warm the Beet Korma in a medium saucepan over medium heat. Spoon onto a large serving plate or individual serving plates. Top with the cauliflower and tofu, and garnish with hemp seeds, if using. Serve immediately with rice or naan.

**NOTE**
I recommend using super firm tofu, also sold as pressed or high protein tofu, for this recipe. If you can't find super firm tofu, you can press extra firm tofu at home (see page 20).

# BEET KORMA PASTA

*with Lemony Garlic Breadcrumbs*

Serves 4 as a main

Don't know what to do with leftover korma (or any curry)? Throw in some pasta (any type you like), and you're good to go for a meal. I chose to feature my Beet Korma (page 63) with pasta here because it's a showstopper. I top it off with panko breadcrumbs, which are infused with lemon and garlic and studded with cumin, for a textural contrast to the smooth and creamy sauce. This topping is universally good for any of the other curry-turned-pasta sauces from this chapter. This pasta pairs very well with Roasted Vegetables with Green Chutney Tahini Sauce (page 101).

**BREADCRUMBS**

1 tablespoon olive oil
2 garlic cloves, minced (about 2 teaspoons)
½ teaspoon cumin seeds
½ cup (40 g) panko breadcrumbs
Zest of 1 lemon (about 1 teaspoon)

**PASTA**

1 pound (454 g) dry pasta
Salt
1 batch Beet Korma (page 63)

1. Bring a large pot of water to a boil.
2. Meanwhile, make the breadcrumbs: Heat the oil in a medium pan over medium heat. Add the garlic and cumin seeds, and stir until just fragrant, about 30 seconds. Add the panko and toast, stirring frequently, until evenly golden brown, 2 to 3 minutes. Stir in the lemon zest and transfer to a small bowl to prevent over-browning.
3. Season the boiling water generously with salt, and then add the pasta and cook according to the package instructions, reserving about ½ cup (120 ml) of pasta water.
4. While the pasta is cooking, warm the Beet Korma in a large saucepan over medium heat. Drain and add the pasta, and mix well to combine. Add pasta water if needed to achieve a saucy consistency. Taste and adjust for salt.
5. Transfer the pasta to serving bowls, top with the breadcrumbs, and serve immediately.

# MADRAS CURRY

Makes 3½ cups (840 ml)

Madras—now officially known as Chennai—is a bustling metropolis in the South Indian state of Tamil Nadu. In the West, "Madras curry" has come to represent a simplified, one-size-fits-all take on South Indian curries, which typically features onions, tomatoes, and curry powder (more about curry powder on page 17). Though you can typically find jarred "Madras curry" in the supermarket, the flavor is often too dull or one-note from the chili or tomato.

I hesitated to call this recipe "Madras Curry" because the term is so vague and can easily oversimplify the rich diversity of South Indian coastal cuisines. This version is my way of reclaiming the name and crafting a more nuanced tribute to the vibrant flavors of South India and Sri Lanka. In this curry, I bring together hallmark ingredients from these regions—creamy coconut, fragrant onions, mustard seeds, aromatic curry leaves, and a pinch of asafetida.

1 tablespoon neutral oil
1 teaspoon mustard seeds
15 fresh curry leaves, thinly sliced
Pinch of asafetida, optional
1 large red onion, finely diced (about 2 cups/300 g)
Salt
9 garlic cloves, minced (about 3 tablespoons)
1 tablespoon minced ginger
3 tablespoons double concentrated tomato paste
1 tablespoon ground coriander
1 tablespoon curry powder
½ teaspoon ground red chili, plus more to taste
Freshly cracked black pepper, to taste
One 13.5-ounce (400 ml) can coconut milk

1. Heat the oil in a large pot over medium heat. Add the mustard seeds and cook until they start to pop and splutter, 30 to 60 seconds. Add the curry leaves and asafetida, if using, and stir until the spluttering subsides, 30 to 60 seconds.
2. Add the onions and ½ teaspoon salt, and cook, stirring frequently with a wooden spoon, until translucent and evenly browned, about 8 minutes. Reduce the heat slightly if needed to prevent the onions from burning.
3. Reduce the heat to medium-low and add the garlic and ginger. Stir until fragrant, about 2 minutes.
4. Add the tomato paste, coriander, curry powder, chili, and black pepper and ½ teaspoon salt, and stir frequently until deepened in color, about 5 minutes. Add water, 1 to 2 tablespoons at a time, to prevent sticking and burning, if needed.
5. Stir in the coconut milk and 1½ cups (360 ml) water and bring to a simmer. Simmer until thickened but still pourable and deep orange-red in color, 10 to 15 minutes. Taste and adjust for salt and heat (chili).
6. Serve as desired or store in an airtight container in the refrigerator for up to 5 days. This is particularly good the next day, once the flavors have had a chance to meld further after a night or two in the fridge.

# MADRAS CAULIFLOWER

Serves 2 to 4 as a main

I love cauliflower in all forms, but roasting is my favorite application. The cauliflower becomes perfectly tender and slightly sweet, and the charred bits make it crave-worthy. In Indian cuisine, cauliflower—known as gobi—is a beloved staple, often featured in dishes like aloo gobi (potatoes and cauliflower), gobi Manchurian (see page 136), and spiced stir fries. When paired with my Madras Curry (page 70), it's a hearty veg-forward meal with minimal effort.

1 large head cauliflower, cut into florets
1 to 2 tablespoons olive oil
1 teaspoon curry powder
Salt
1 batch Madras Curry (page 70)

**FOR SERVING**

Microgreens or chopped fresh cilantro leaves, optional
Fluffy Basmati Rice (page 154) or Homestyle Indian Fried Rice (page 169)

1 Preheat the oven to 425°F (220°C). Line 2 sheet pans with parchment paper (if desired, for easier cleanup).

2 Place the cauliflower in a single layer on the sheet pans. Drizzle the oil onto the cauliflower and sprinkle with the curry powder and salt to taste. Massage the oil into the cauliflower pieces and roast for 15 to 20 minutes, until tender and browned on the edges.

3 When the cauliflower is almost done cooking, warm the Madras Curry in a large saucepan over medium heat. Transfer the curry to a serving bowl. Top with the roasted cauliflower and microgreens, if using, and serve immediately with rice.

# SEARED MAITAKE MUSHROOMS

## *with Madras Curry*

Serves 2 to 4 as a main

I love the umami and earthiness that mushrooms provide, and one of my favorite varieties is maitake (also known as hen of the woods). In Japanese, maitake means "dancing mushroom," a reference to the almost feathery, "dancing" appearance of the mushroom. Not much needs to be done to the magnificent maitake, since it's really a showpiece in and of itself. It has been used for centuries in Japanese and Chinese cuisines in hot pots, stir fries, and soups. Here, I've seared maitake mushrooms to make the perfect vehicle for sopping up my Madras Curry (page 70), with crispy edges and a pleasantly chewy interior. If you can get your hands on a good maitake (use it the same day you buy it), you must try this recipe. But if you can't, you can most definitely use any other mushroom you like, such as oyster, portobello, or cremini.

1 tablespoon olive oil
8 ounces (227 g) maitake mushrooms, cut into large chunks
Salt
Freshly cracked black pepper
1 batch Madras Curry (page 70)
Fluffy Basmati Rice (page 154) or Flaky Scallion Paratha (page 181), optional, for serving

1. Heat the oil in a large skillet over medium heat. Add the mushrooms and sear until browned on both sides, about 5 minutes per side, pressing the mushrooms onto the pan to flatten and allow more surface area to crisp.
2. Season the mushrooms with salt and black pepper to taste.
3. Warm the Madras Curry in a medium saucepan over medium heat and then spread it evenly onto a serving plate. Top with the mushrooms and enjoy with rice, scallion paratha, or on its own.

# GARLICKY CAULIFLOWER PUREE

Makes 4 cups (960 ml)

Even simple purees can be used like a curry. Cauliflower, when boiled and blended, can be more than just baby food. It becomes a silky, nuanced sauce—think of this like a vegan, Indian-ish take on a béchamel, a French mother sauce made from a roux (flour and butter) and milk. Here, without the flour and dairy, it maintains its consistency well, so it's very forgiving to make. The combination of cumin, peppercorns, asafetida, and garlic gives it an Indian flair, which allows it to pair well with the recipes that follow.

2 tablespoons olive oil
½ teaspoon cumin seeds
½ teaspoon black peppercorns
6 garlic cloves, minced (about 2 tablespoons)
Pinch of asafetida
1 medium head cauliflower, leaves removed, stem trimmed, and cut into small pieces (4 to 5 cups/600 g)
1 or 2 bay leaves
Salt

1. Heat the oil in a large saucepan over medium heat. Add the cumin seeds and peppercorns and stir until fragrant, a few seconds.
2. Add the garlic and asafetida and stir until fragrant and barely starting to brown, about 1 minute.
3. Add the cauliflower, bay leaves, ¾ teaspoon salt, and just enough water to cover (about 2 cups/480 ml), and simmer until the cauliflower is very soft, about 20 minutes. Remove from the heat and allow to cool.
4. Discard the bay leaves and transfer the cooked cauliflower and spices to a blender using a slotted spoon, reserving any cooking liquid. Blend until silky smooth, adding back cooking liquid as needed to aid in blending. Taste and adjust for salt.
5. Serve as desired or store in an airtight container in the refrigerator for up to 3 days or in the freezer for up to 3 months.

# BRAISED MISO TOFU AND ONIONS

## *with Cauliflower Puree*

Serves 2 to 3 as a main

Braising tofu is a technique used in both Chinese and Korean cuisines; braising makes the tofu amazingly toothsome, while also infusing each bite with the flavor of the broth. First, the tofu is pan-fried until browned and then it's simmered in a savory, salty, and often spicy broth. Here, I take this traditional East Asian technique and add Indian spices (curry powder and garam masala), Western flavors (Dijon mustard, balsamic vinegar, and maple syrup), and miso for umami. The result is a tofu that has warmth from the spices, heat from the Dijon, tang from the balsamic, and sweetness from the maple. My Garlicky Cauliflower Puree (page 77) is a mellow base that soaks up the flavors of the braising liquid, which becomes a rich sauce through the cooking process.

### BRAISING LIQUID

1 cup (240 ml) low-sodium vegetable broth
2 tablespoons white miso
2 tablespoons nutritional yeast, optional (see Note)
1 tablespoon balsamic vinegar
1 tablespoon Dijon mustard
1 teaspoon maple syrup
½ teaspoon curry powder
½ teaspoon garam masala
Freshly cracked black pepper, to taste

### ONIONS AND TOFU

2 tablespoons olive oil, divided
1 small white onion, thinly sliced (about 1 cup/150 g)
Salt
3 garlic cloves, minced (about 1 tablespoon)
1½ teaspoons minced ginger
One 14-ounce (397 g) block extra firm tofu, drained

### FOR SERVING

½ batch Garlicky Cauliflower Puree (page 77)
Chopped fresh cilantro leaves or flat-leaf parsley

1 Prepare the braising liquid: Combine the broth, miso, nutritional yeast (if using), balsamic vinegar, mustard, maple syrup, curry powder, garam masala, and black pepper in a medium bowl. Stir until smooth.

2 Cook the onions: Heat 1 tablespoon oil in a large nonstick pan over medium heat. Add the onions and ¼ teaspoon salt, and stir until the onions soften and start to brown, about 8 minutes. Add the garlic and ginger, and stir until fragrant, about 1 minute. Transfer the onions and garlic to a bowl.

3 Prepare the tofu: Cut the tofu into six ¾-inch (2 cm) thick slices and pat dry with a clean kitchen towel. Cut the slices in half to form squares.

4 Heat the remaining 1 tablespoon oil in the same large nonstick pan over medium-high heat. Add the tofu in an even layer. Cook until browned, about 8 minutes on each side.

5 Add the onions and braising liquid to the pan. Simmer until the liquid becomes a thick sauce, about 10 minutes.

6 While the tofu is simmering, warm the Garlicky Cauliflower Puree in a small saucepan over medium heat.

7 Distribute the cauliflower puree evenly among two or three plates. Top each plate with four or six slices of tofu and some onions and braising sauce. Garnish with cilantro and serve immediately.

### NOTE

Nutritional yeast is not the same as yeast used for baking. It is an inactive yeast that is often used in vegan cooking to add a cheesy flavor. Many nutritional yeast brands are also fortified with B vitamins, providing an added nutrient boost. If you can't find it, simply omit.

# FETTUCCINE

## *in Tadka Cauliflower Sauce*

Serves 2 to 3 as a main

I can't think of fettuccine Alfredo without thinking about Olive Garden, the nostalgic Italian American (well, mostly American) casual dining restaurant chain. Whenever I went there, whether it was a special weekend treat with my family or my freshman year homecoming dinner with friends, fettuccine Alfredo was always on the table. The dish was incredibly rich, yet we couldn't get enough of the creamy, salty flavor. I've since developed a lighter, dairy-free version that's just as delicious. My Garlicky Cauliflower Puree (page 77) is a great mellow pasta sauce on its own, but adding a tadka (spices and aromatics bloomed in oil) really takes it over the top.

Salt
8 ounces (227 g) dry fettuccine
¼ batch (240 ml) Garlicky Cauliflower Puree (page 77)
1 tablespoon olive oil
½ teaspoon cumin seeds
½ to 1 teaspoon gochugaru or crushed red pepper flakes
Pinch of asafetida, optional
10 fresh curry leaves, thinly sliced

1. Bring a large pot of water to a boil. Season generously with salt and then add the pasta and cook according to the package instructions, reserving about ½ cup (120 ml) pasta water.
2. While the pasta is cooking, warm the Garlicky Cauliflower Puree in a large saucepan over medium heat. Add the pasta and mix well to combine. Add pasta water if needed to achieve a saucy consistency. Taste and adjust for salt.
3. Heat the oil in a small saucepan over medium heat. Add the cumin seeds and heat until fragrant and starting to brown, about 1 minute. Add the gochugaru and asafetida, if using, and then turn off the heat. Add the curry leaves and stir until crisp, a few seconds. Use a spoon to pour the mixture evenly over the pasta, and serve immediately.

# CHUTNEYS, DIPS, DRESSINGS, AND MORE!

Where the previous chapter focused on rich and creamy curries, this chapter includes lighter non-curry sauces that come together a bit more quickly. These recipes highlight just how versatile and powerful a good sauce can be. You'll find options that anchor hearty stand-alone meals like my Lemon Pepper Glaze (page 145), which pairs perfectly with tofu and broccoli. You'll also find others that double as dressings for grain bowls or salads and some that are perfect as dips or punchy sides to round out a plate. These sauces borrow ingredients and techniques from various corners of India and across Asia.

Whether you're looking to upgrade leftovers, bring new life to roasted veggies, or throw together a quick dinner with pantry staples, these sauces are designed to support you with bold flavor and little fuss. They're the unsung heroes that make even the simplest meals shine.

# MANGO MISO MASALA CHUTNEY

Makes 2¼ cups (540 ml)

A good mango chutney needs a balance of flavor—sweetness from mango, heat from chili, and nuance from masala (spices and aromatics, such as ginger and cumin). Since this sweet-leaning chutney is usually paired with savory foods, I add miso, Japanese fermented soybean paste, to bring out the savory notes further.

While fresh mango is wonderful, this is one of the only cases where frozen mango is actually better—it allows you to make this recipe year-round, so you can save those juicy peak-season mangoes for eating. This chutney adds a burst of tropical brightness to just about anything and is a classic companion to snacks like pakoras (page 89) and samosas. If you don't have the time (or desire) to make your own samosas, there's no shame in buying frozen ones or ordering them from your favorite Indian takeout spot. Once this chutney is on the plate, it'll steal the show anyway.

1 tablespoon olive oil
2 garlic cloves, minced (about 2 teaspoons)
2 teaspoons minced ginger
1 teaspoon coriander seeds
1 teaspoon cumin seeds
1 teaspoon fennel seeds
2 cups (280 g) frozen mango chunks
3 tablespoons maple syrup
¼ teaspoon ground red chili
¼ teaspoon garam masala
¼ teaspoon ground turmeric
Salt
1 tablespoon white miso

1. Heat the oil in a large saucepan over medium heat. Add the garlic and ginger and cook, stirring frequently, until fragrant and softened, about 2 minutes.
2. Add the coriander seeds, cumin seeds, and fennel seeds, and stir until fragrant and starting to brown, about 30 seconds.
3. Add the mango, maple syrup, chili, garam masala, turmeric, ½ teaspoon salt, and 1½ cups (360 ml) water, and stir well to combine.
4. Simmer until the mango is easily mashed with a fork, about 5 minutes.
5. Let cool. Then transfer to a blender, add the miso, and blend until completely smooth. Taste and adjust for salt.
6. Serve as desired, or store in a glass jar or squeeze bottle in the refrigerator for up to 5 days or in an airtight container in the freezer for up to 3 months.

NOTES

1 Ajwain seeds, which provide an herbal, thyme-like flavor, are often found in pakoras (see page 94 for another pakora recipe). It's worth buying a small quantity to try.

2 These pakoras can be made up to 2 hours ahead and reheated in the oven on a parchment paper-lined sheet pan at 400°F (200°C) for about 5 minutes, until crisp and heated through.

# ZUCCHINI CORN PAKORAS

## *with Mango Miso Masala Chutney*

Serves 4 as an appetizer or snack

Pakoras are beloved crispy Indian snacks typically made by coating vegetables in a spiced besan (or chickpea flour) batter and frying them until golden and crunchy. They're often served with a bold chutney on the side and are a staple during the monsoon season, but they're also great whenever you need a savory snack.

In our family, pakoras are more than just a snack—they're a tradition. Every summer, my mom pulls out her portable gas stove and hosts a backyard "pakora party" for friends and family. It's a joyful, slightly chaotic affair with heaps of cauliflower, kale, onions, tofu, and whatever else we feel like dunking into the batter. These gatherings, always full of laughter and hot oil pops, inspired this recipe.

These pakoras feature some of my favorite summer produce—onions, zucchini, and sweet corn—which come together in a crisp, golden fritter that's deeply satisfying yet light enough to enjoy in warm weather. If you ever find yourself wondering what to do with that haul of farmers market veggies (or an unfamiliar squash that showed up in your CSA box), making pakoras is generally a good move. When paired with my Mango Miso Masala Chutney (page 86), they become a true celebration of summer. This recipe was an instant hit with this book's editor, Olivia, and DK's editorial director, Ann, when I had the pleasure of having them taste-test it.

1 large zucchini, cut into thin matchsticks (about 3 cups/300 g)
1 small red onion, thinly sliced (about 1 cup/150 g)
1 cup (125 g) fresh or frozen corn kernels
2 to 3 scallions, thinly sliced
Salt
2 garlic cloves, minced (about 2 teaspoons)
2 teaspoons minced ginger
½ teaspoon cumin seeds
¼ teaspoon ajwain (carom) seeds, optional (see Note 1)
Freshly cracked black pepper, to taste
½ cup (60 g) besan or chickpea flour, plus more as needed
Neutral oil, for frying

### FOR SERVING

Chaat masala or salt, optional
Chopped fresh cilantro leaves, optional
½ cup (120 ml) Mango Miso Masala Chutney (page 86)

1. Combine the zucchini, onions, corn, and scallions and ¾ teaspoon salt in a large bowl, massaging the salt evenly into the vegetables with clean hands. Set aside for about 10 minutes, squeezing the vegetables every few minutes, until the vegetables release liquid and feel wet; you may see about 1 tablespoon liquid accumulating at the bottom of the bowl.
2. Stir in the garlic, ginger, cumin seeds, ajwain seeds (if using), and black pepper. Incorporate the besan with clean fingers, 1 tablespoon at a time, until the mixture just starts holding together and the vegetables are thinly and evenly coated in the batter. Add a sprinkling of water with your fingers if the mixture is too dry.
3. Place a cooling rack on top of a paper towel-lined baking sheet (for easier cleanup).
4. Heat about ½ inch (1 cm) oil to 350°F (180°C) in a large skillet over medium heat. You'll know the oil is ready when you place a small amount of the pakora batter into the oil and it sizzles immediately.
5. Working in batches, place small heaps (2 to 3 tablespoons each) of the pakora mixture in the skillet, 1 to 2 inches (2.5 to 5 cm) apart, and flatten slightly. Cook until the pakoras start to brown on the bottom, 3 to 4 minutes. Flip and flatten slightly, and cook until browned on the other side, 3 to 4 minutes.
6. Transfer to the cooling rack to drain any excess oil. Top with a light sprinkle of chaat masala and cilantro, if using. Serve immediately with the chutney (see Note 2).

# MANGO MISO MASALA GLAZED CAULIFLOWER

## *with Quinoa*

Serves 2 to 4 as a main

Mango Miso Masala Chutney (page 86) can be more than just a dipping sauce. Here, it becomes a glaze that caramelizes in the oven on top of perfectly charred and tender cauliflower. You can also use this same technique for glazing other vegetables, tofu, or tempeh. I like to pair this combination with quinoa to make it more of a complete meal, but feel free to serve it on its own as a side or with rice.

This recipe is a great example of how a bold, well-balanced condiment can completely transform your vegetables—and a delicious reminder that cauliflower doesn't need to be a supporting player. With a little help from a good glaze, it can absolutely be the star.

1 large head cauliflower, cut into thick slices
1 to 2 tablespoons olive oil
Salt
Mango Miso Masala Chutney (page 86), to taste

**FOR SERVING**

2 cups (370 g) cooked quinoa
Microgreens, optional

1. Preheat the oven to 425°F (220°C). Line 2 sheet pans with parchment paper (if desired, for easier cleanup).
2. Place the cauliflower in a single layer on the sheet pans. Drizzle oil onto the cauliflower and sprinkle with a light pinch of salt (don't add too much, since the chutney is seasoned). Massage the oil into the cauliflower pieces and roast for 20 to 25 minutes, until tender and browned on the edges.
3. Brush the cauliflower generously on all sides with Mango Miso Masala Chutney to taste. Return to the oven and roast for 5 minutes, until the glaze is glossy and starts to caramelize.
4. Serve the cauliflower over quinoa and top with microgreens, if desired.

# CRANBERRY CHUTNEY

Makes 1 cup (240 ml)

Typically made from tamarind and/or dates, sweet chutney is a sauce that's often served alongside samosas (usually with a green chutney; see page 98) and other Indian snack foods. But tamarind can be difficult to find. Enter this cranberry chutney, a nod to my Wisconsin upbringing, as the state is one of the top cranberry producers in the US. Cranberries have a vibrant red hue, and their tart brightness mimics tamarind remarkably well. In this sauce, I round it all out with warm spices and just enough maple syrup to balance the sourness.

You can find bags of cranberries in the freezer section of the grocery store year-round—or you can stock up when they're in season in the fall and freeze them yourself. And if cranberries aren't available to you at all, fresh or frozen raspberries make a solid substitute. Just be sure to reduce the sweetener a bit (start with ¼ cup/60 ml and add more to taste) since raspberries are naturally sweeter.

½ teaspoon coriander seeds
½ teaspoon cumin seeds
½ teaspoon fennel seeds
1 cup (100 g) frozen or fresh cranberries
½ cup (120 ml) maple syrup or cane sugar
¼ teaspoon ground red chili
Salt

1. Heat the coriander seeds, cumin seeds, and fennel seeds in a large saucepan over medium heat. Stir until fragrant and just starting to brown, about 1 minute.
2. Add the cranberries, maple syrup, chili, ½ teaspoon salt, and 1 cup (240 ml) water, and stir to combine. Bring to a boil and then reduce the heat to maintain a simmer.
3. Simmer until the cranberries are easily mashed with a fork and the liquid is syrupy in consistency, about 10 minutes.
4. Let cool, transfer to a blender, and blend until smooth. Thin with water, 1 tablespoon at a time, if the chutney becomes too thick. Taste and adjust for salt.
5. Serve as desired, or store in a glass jar or squeeze bottle in the refrigerator for up to 5 days or in an airtight container in the freezer for up to 3 months.

# BRUSSELS SPROUT PAKORAS

## *with Cranberry Chutney*

Serves 4 to 6 as an appetizer or snack

Both brussels sprouts and cranberries remind me of fall in the Midwest, where I was born and raised. To this day, my parents host Thanksgiving at their home in Wisconsin for up to 30 members of our extended family. The main meal rarely includes what might be considered traditional Thanksgiving food; instead, we eat whatever the family is in the mood for that day. One year, it was stuffed pasta shells with marinara sauce; another year it was chhole (spiced chickpeas)—and there are always tons of appetizers and sides.

This dish follows that same spirit. Turning brussels sprouts into pakoras and cranberries into chutney might not be traditional—these ingredients aren't typically found in Indian cuisine—but neither are the Thanksgivings I grew up with. Whether you serve this dish at a holiday gathering or just to enjoy fall produce, it's a celebration of both season and family with no boundaries required.

7 ounces (198 g) brussels sprouts, trimmed and thinly sliced lengthwise (about 2 cups)
1 small red onion, quartered and then thinly sliced (about 1 cup/150 g)
Salt
2 garlic cloves, minced (about 2 teaspoons)
1½ teaspoons chopped fresh rosemary leaves (see Note 1)
½ teaspoon cumin seeds
½ teaspoon ground turmeric
¼ teaspoon ajwain (carom) seeds, optional (see Note on page 88)
Freshly cracked black pepper, to taste
½ cup (60 g) besan or chickpea flour, plus more as needed
Neutral oil, for frying
Chaat masala, optional, for serving
½ batch Cranberry Chutney (page 93), for serving

1 Combine the brussels sprouts, onions, and ¾ teaspoon salt in a large bowl, massaging the salt evenly into the vegetables with clean hands. Let sit for about 10 minutes, squeezing the vegetables every few minutes, until they release liquid and feel wet.

2 Stir in the garlic, rosemary, cumin seeds, turmeric, ajwain seeds (if using), and black pepper. Incorporate the besan with clean fingers, 1 tablespoon at a time, until the mixture just starts holding together and the vegetables are thinly and evenly coated in the batter. Add a sprinkling of water with your fingers if the mixture is too dry.

3 Place a cooling rack on top of a paper towel-lined baking sheet (for easier cleanup).

4 Heat about 1 inch (2.5 cm) oil to 325°F (165°C) in a medium wok or small Dutch oven over medium heat (see Note 2). You'll know the oil is ready when you place a small amount of the pakora batter into the oil and it sizzles immediately.

5 Working in batches, place small heaps (about 1 to 2 tablespoons each) of the pakora mixture into the oil, 1 to 2 inches (2.5 to 5 cm) apart. Cook until evenly browned, flipping as needed to ensure even browning on all sides, 2 to 4 minutes.

6 Use a spider strainer to transfer the pakoras to the cooling rack to drain any excess oil. Top with a light sprinkle of chaat masala, if using, or salt. Serve immediately with Cranberry Chutney (see Note 3).

**NOTES**

1 You won't find rosemary in traditional pakora recipes, but it complements the cranberry chutney well here! It's not totally essential, so don't feel like you need to get it just for this recipe (but if you do, you can use the leftover rosemary in my French Lentils on page 162).

2 These pakoras can also be fried in a pan with less oil, using the same method from my Zucchini Corn Pakoras (page 89).

3 These pakoras can be made up to 2 hours ahead and reheated in the oven on a parchment paper-lined sheet pan at 400°F (200°C) for about 5 minutes, until crisp and heated through.

# GREEN PEA TIKKIS

## *with Cranberry Chutney*

Makes about 25 tikkis

This recipe takes inspiration from hara bhara kebab, a popular North Indian appetizer made with mashed potatoes, green peas, herbs, and warming spices. My version of these tikkis (patties) is packed with bold aromatics—whole cumin and fennel seeds add a toasty depth and gentle sweetness, while jalapeño, garlic, and ginger bring just the right amount of heat. With the addition of panko for texture, the result is a tikki that achieves a perfect balance of crispness on the outside and tenderness on the inside.

I pair these tikkis with my tangy-sweet Cranberry Chutney (page 93), which adds brightness, a pop of color, and just enough acidity to balance the spices. While the tikkis and chutney are a standout snack on their own, they're also incredibly versatile: Tuck them into a wrap with crunchy lettuce and pickled onions or pair them with a curry sauce from chapter 1 for a hearty meal.

- 1 large russet potato, quartered (about 325 g)
- Salt
- 1½ cups (195 g) frozen peas
- 1½ cups (120 g) panko breadcrumbs, divided
- 1 jalapeño, seeded for milder spice, minced
- ¼ cup (7 g) chopped fresh mint and/or cilantro leaves
- 3 garlic cloves, minced (about 1 tablespoon)
- 1 tablespoon minced ginger
- 1 teaspoon garam masala
- ½ teaspoon chaat masala, plus more to taste
- ½ teaspoon cumin seeds
- ½ teaspoon fennel seeds
- Neutral oil, for frying

**FOR SERVING**

- Microgreens or chopped fresh herbs (such as cilantro or mint)
- ½ batch Cranberry Chutney (page 93)

1. Place the potatoes in a medium saucepan with about 1 teaspoon salt and about 5 cups (1.2 L) water, covering the potatoes by 1 to 2 inches (2.5 to 5 cm). Bring to a boil over high heat, reduce the heat to maintain a simmer, and cook until you can insert a fork into the potatoes with minimal resistance, about 12 minutes.
2. Remove from the heat and use tongs or a slotted spoon to transfer the potatoes to a large bowl to cool slightly.
3. Place the peas in the hot water and allow them to thaw in the residual heat until tender, 1 to 2 minutes. Transfer to a strainer to drain the hot water, rinse under cold water to cool, and drain the excess water. Pat with a clean kitchen towel to remove excess moisture and then transfer to a small food processor. Pulse to form a coarse paste.
4. Remove and discard the potato skins and mash the potatoes until no large chunks remain. Add the peas, 1 cup (80 g) panko, and the jalapeño, mint, garlic, ginger, garam masala, chaat masala, cumin seeds, and fennel seeds. Mix with clean hands to form a cohesive mixture. Mix in more salt, if needed, to taste.
5. To form the tikkis, place the remaining ½ cup (40 g) panko in a small bowl. Take 1½ tablespoons of the tikki mixture (I like using a cookie scoop for this) and form it into a tightly packed ball with your hands. Flatten slightly and then press both sides gently into the panko to coat. Transfer to a large tray or plate.
6. Place a cooling rack on top of a paper towel-lined baking sheet.
7. Heat about ½ inch (1 cm) oil to 350°F (180°C) in a large skillet over medium heat. You'll know the oil is ready when you place a pinch of breadcrumbs into the oil and it sizzles immediately.
8. Working in two or three batches, add the tikkis and fry until golden brown, 3 to 4 minutes per side. Transfer to the cooling rack to drain any excess oil. Sprinkle with chaat masala to taste.
9. Transfer the cooked tikkis to a serving plate, top with microgreens, and serve immediately with Cranberry Chutney.

# GREEN CHUTNEY TAHINI SAUCE

Makes 1⅓ cups (320 ml)

The unfortunate truth about many green chutneys is that they can be watery and underwhelming. But with just one creamy, cohesive ingredient—tahini—they can transform. Tahini gives this chutney body, richness, and a slightly nutty backdrop that complements the bold flavors of herbs, citrus, and chili beautifully. The result is a vibrant, creamy green chutney that doesn't just sit on the plate—it brings everything else to life. This chutney is all about balance, so be generous—but thoughtful—with the green chili and lime juice. If you're not into tahini or don't have any on hand, you can easily swap in cashews, roasted peanuts, hemp seeds, or even silken tofu for a similarly creamy consistency. The green chili variety is up to you: Go with jalapeño (seeded), if you want it mild, serrano for medium heat, or Thai green chili if you're ready to turn things up a notch. Tahini can sometimes be a bit bitter, so if you find this is the case with your chutney, simply amp up the lime juice and chaat masala to balance it out.

1 cup (60 g) packed fresh cilantro leaves and stems
½ cup (65 g) tahini
½ cup (14 g) packed fresh mint leaves
1 green chili, sliced, or to taste (see Headnote)
2½ tablespoons lime juice (from about 1 large lime), plus more to taste
2 garlic cloves, minced (about 2 teaspoons)
2 teaspoons minced ginger
1 teaspoon chaat masala, plus more to taste
Salt

1. Combine the cilantro, tahini, mint, chili, lime juice, garlic, ginger, chaat masala, ½ teaspoon salt, and ½ cup plus 2 tablespoons (150 ml) water in a blender. Blend until smooth and taste for salt, umami (chaat masala), acid (lime juice), and heat (chili).
2. Serve as desired, or store in a glass jar or squeeze bottle in the refrigerator for up to 5 days or in an airtight container in the freezer for up to 3 months.

# ROASTED VEGETABLES

*with Green Chutney Tahini Sauce*

Serves 2 to 4

Roasting is hands down one of my favorite ways to cook vegetables. It's a low-effort, high-reward technique that never fails to deliver. A good roast coaxes out the natural sweetness in vegetables, creates those crisp golden edges everyone fights over, and adds a gentle smokiness that's hard to beat. In this recipe, I pair caramelized veggies with a generous drizzle of my Green Chutney Tahini Sauce (page 98), which punches up the flavor and makes the whole thing feel a little more special.

Think of this less as a strict recipe and more as a framework. You can roast just about any veg you've got lying around—cauliflower, carrots, sweet potatoes, brussels sprouts, broccoli, zucchini, or even wedges of cabbage. Just chop, toss with oil and salt, and let the oven do the work. It's also an excellent meal prep component; roast a big tray of veg and keep the sauce in the fridge to jazz up bowls, wraps, or salads throughout the week. Whether you serve it as a side, a light main, or as part of a larger spread, this roasted veg + chutney combo is endlessly adaptable.

1 medium red bell pepper, cut into bite-size pieces
1 medium head broccoli, cut into bite-size florets
1 large carrot, cut into bite-size pieces
1 small head cauliflower, cut into bite-size florets
1 large zucchini, cut into bite-size pieces
2 tablespoons olive oil, plus more for serving
Freshly cracked black pepper, to taste
Salt, to taste
½ batch Green Chutney Tahini Sauce (page 98)
1 tablespoon toasted sesame seeds, optional, for serving

1. Preheat the oven to 425°F (220°C). Line 2 sheet pans with parchment paper (if desired, for easier cleanup).
2. Place the bell peppers, broccoli, carrots, cauliflower, and zucchini in an even layer on the sheet pans. Drizzle with the oil and sprinkle with salt and black pepper. Massage the oil into the vegetables.
3. Roast for about 20 minutes, or until the vegetables are tender and starting to brown.
4. To serve, spread the Green Chutney Tahini Sauce on a large platter with a spoon or squeeze bottle. Top with the roasted vegetables, a drizzle of oil, sesame seeds (if using), and black pepper, and serve immediately or at room temperature.

# CRISPY CHICKPEA SALAD

## *with Green Chutney Tahini Sauce*

Serves 2 as a main or 4 as a side

Chickpeas play a starring role in many versions of chaat, a beloved Indian street snack that layers crunchy, tangy, and spicy flavors over bases of potatoes, samosas, chickpeas, or puffed rice. Typically, chaat is topped with a symphony of chutneys, diced onions, and fresh vegetables and finished with a sprinkle of chaat masala—an addictive spice blend featuring amchur (dry mango powder) and black salt that gives it that signature tang.

This chaat-inspired salad takes all of those bold flavors and transforms them into a fresh, nourishing bowl. It features a generous heap of crisp greens and vibrant veggies, topped with crispy chickpeas dusted with chaat masala for that irresistible crunch and tang. To tie it all together, I drizzle it with Green Chutney Tahini Sauce (page 98), which adds a bright, herbaceous lift. It's a fresh, fun way to enjoy all the addictive flavors of chaat in a lighter salad form.

- One 16-ounce (454 g) can chickpeas, drained and rinsed
- 1 to 2 tablespoons olive oil
- Freshly cracked black pepper, to taste
- Salt, to taste
- ½ teaspoon chaat masala, plus more to taste
- 4 to 5 ounces (113 to 142 g) mixed leafy greens, torn or roughly chopped
- 1 small avocado, sliced
- ½ medium English cucumber, sliced
- ¼ small purple cabbage, thinly sliced
- ¼ cup (60 ml) Green Chutney Tahini Sauce (page 98), or to taste
- 2 to 3 tablespoons sunflower seeds
- 1 tablespoon toasted sesame seeds

1. Preheat the oven to 425°F (220°C). Line a sheet pan with parchment paper.
2. Dry the chickpeas thoroughly with a clean kitchen towel. Transfer to the sheet pan. Coat the chickpeas evenly with the oil and sprinkle with a pinch of salt and black pepper. Spread the chickpeas into an even layer and bake for 30 minutes, or until crunchy (keeping in mind they will crisp as they cool). Sprinkle with the chaat masala.
3. Arrange the greens, avocado, cucumber, and cabbage in a large serving bowl or two smaller bowls, and drizzle with the Green Chutney Tahini Sauce. Top with the chickpeas, sunflower seeds, sesame seeds, and more black pepper and chaat masala, if desired. Serve immediately.

# CHILI LIME TADKA DRESSING

Makes ½ cup (120 ml)

Tadka, the process of blooming whole and/or ground spices and herbs in hot oil, is a South Asian cooking technique that results in a deeply perfumed oil that can completely transform the flavor of a dish. Here, I've turned a simple yet very aromatic tadka into a dressing that features the bright zing of fresh lime, the subtly smoky heat of gochugaru, the depth and gentle bitterness of mustard seeds, and the umami-rich, oniony notes of asafetida. Fresh curry leaves add a lively herbaceous brightness, while a touch of maple syrup balances everything with a hint of sweetness. This versatile dressing is perfect for drizzling over salads (like the Endive Apple Salad on page 108), adding a punch to sandwiches, or elevating wraps. It's a simple way to bring the magic of tadka into your everyday meals.

- ½ teaspoon lime zest (from about 1 lime)
- ¼ cup (60 ml) lime juice (from 2 to 3 limes), plus more to taste
- 1 tablespoon maple syrup, plus more to taste
- Salt
- 3 tablespoons olive oil
- ½ teaspoon black mustard seeds
- ¼ teaspoon asafetida
- 15 to 20 fresh curry leaves, thinly sliced, torn, or whole (see Note)
- 2 teaspoons gochugaru or crushed red pepper flakes, to taste

1. Whisk together the lime zest and juice, the maple syrup, and ½ teaspoon salt in a small bowl.
2. Heat the oil in a small saucepan over medium heat. Add the mustard seeds and cook until the seeds begin to pop, about 30 seconds. Add the asafetida and remove from the heat.
3. Immediately add the curry leaves and cook in the hot oil until the spluttering subsides, about 30 seconds. Swirl in the gochugaru and then pour on top of the lime juice mixture. Take a moment to enjoy the fantastic sound of sizzling before whisking to combine. Taste and adjust for salt, acid (lime juice), and sweetness (maple syrup).
4. Serve as desired or store in an airtight container in the refrigerator for up to 5 days. When ready to use, let sit at room temperature until the oil liquefies, about 20 minutes.

**NOTE**

I generally prefer to thinly slice curry leaves to get a small burst of flavor in every bite, but if your curry leaves are small and you like the appearance of whole leaves in your final dish, feel free to keep them whole.

# ENDIVE APPLE SALAD

## *with Chili Lime Tadka Dressing*

Serves 2 to 4 as a side

My wife, Rachel, and I love going to our local Chicagoland apple orchards in the late summer and early fall to get the freshest and tastiest apples. A good in-season apple is a perfect treat on its own, though we also love to pair sliced apples with some nut butter for dipping. Sliced sweet and tart apples are the stars of this simple salad recipe, which also features bitter endive and my Chili Lime Tadka Dressing (page 107). It's great all year round but even better if you use apples that you've picked yourself.

3 small heads endive (red and/or green), separated into leaves
1 medium green apple (such as Granny Smith), thinly sliced
1 medium red apple (such as Honeycrisp), thinly sliced
1 batch room-temperature Chili Lime Tadka Dressing (page 107), or to taste
¼ cup (30 g) walnuts, thinly sliced

1 Toss together the endive, apples, and Chili Lime Tadka Dressing in a large bowl. Transfer to a serving platter, if desired. Top with the walnuts and serve immediately.

# ROASTED SQUASH

## *with Chili Lime Tadka Dressing*

Serves 4 as a side

Hard-rind winter squash, such as butternut, acorn, and kabocha, does particularly well in the oven, since it becomes perfectly tender and caramelized as it roasts. The tangy brightness of my Chili Lime Tadka Dressing (page 107) complements this well, and I like to top it off with crispy hand-torn breadcrumbs for a textural delight! This is a great side dish for the fall table, alongside my Beet Korma (page 63).

- 2 acorn squashes, cut into ¾-inch (2 cm) slices and seeds removed
- 1 small butternut squash, cut into ¾-inch (2 cm) slices and seeds removed
- 2 tablespoons olive oil
- Salt
- 1 cup (about 100 g) diced or torn sourdough bread
- 1 batch room-temperature Chili Lime Tadka Dressing (page 107), or to taste

1. Preheat the oven to 425°F (220°C). Line 2 sheet pans with parchment paper.
2. Evenly spread the squash onto the pans. Drizzle with the oil and sprinkle with salt to taste. Massage the oil into the squash and then roast for 30 minutes, or until fork tender and starting to caramelize.
3. While the squash is roasting, toast the bread in a large skillet over medium heat. Stir frequently and cook until crisp and starting to brown, about 5 minutes. Season with a pinch of salt.
4. Transfer the cooked squash to a serving platter. Top with the toasted bread and Chili Lime Tadka Dressing. Serve warm or at room temperature.

# CARROT GINGER DRESSING

Makes 1½ cups (360 ml)

This bright, tangy, and gingery dressing is inspired by the classic carrot ginger salad dressing served at many Japanese American restaurants—a nostalgic favorite known for its bold flavor and vibrant color. To deepen those familiar notes, I add an unexpected (but completely at home) ingredient: curry powder.

Though curry powder didn't originate in Japan, it became a beloved part of Japanese cuisine in the early 20th century, introduced through British colonial influence. One of the most iconic versions—S&B curry powder—has been made in Japan for over a century and is still widely available in Asian grocery stores today. It's this same warm, aromatic blend that defines the comforting flavor of Japanese curry rice (karē raisu). Blooming the curry powder in oil not only enhances this dressing's fragrance and flavor but also lends it a beautiful golden hue and gentle heat.

Unlike traditional versions of carrot ginger dressing that rely on mayonnaise for creaminess, this one uses oil and a touch of miso to create a rich, velvety texture—no mayo required. The result is a zippy dressing that's just as good on salads as it is drizzled over roasted vegetables or used as a dipping sauce. It's a small but flavorful reminder of how culinary traditions evolve and intersect.

2 tablespoons olive oil
1 teaspoon curry powder
2 medium carrots, diced (about 1 cup/140 g)
⅓ cup (80 ml) rice vinegar
2 tablespoons maple syrup
1 to 2 tablespoons minced ginger (see Note)
1 tablespoon white miso
1 garlic clove, minced (about 1 teaspoon)
Salt

1. Heat the oil in a small saucepan over medium heat. Add the curry powder and cook until very fragrant, taking caution not to burn, a few seconds. Remove from the heat.
2. Add the curry powder oil, carrots, rice vinegar, maple syrup, 1 tablespoon ginger, miso, garlic, 2 tablespoons water, and ¼ teaspoon salt to a blender. Blend until smooth. Add more ginger to taste and blend again.
3. Serve as desired or store in an airtight container in the refrigerator for up to 5 days.

**NOTE**
I provide a range of ginger here because it's really to taste. I prefer the full 2 tablespoons for a punchy bite, but you can easily dial back if you want a more mellow dressing.

# EDAMAME AND CRISP LETTUCE SALAD

*with Carrot Ginger Dressing*

Serves 2 to 4 as an appetizer or side

Edamame—young, green soybeans—is one of my family's favorite go-to side dishes at our neighborhood sushi spot. Lightly salted and served warm, it's simple, satiating, and packed with protein. So, it felt natural for me to build this Japanese-inspired salad around edamame, especially since frozen edamame is so easy to keep on hand and takes only minutes to prepare.

Here, I pair it with crisp vegetables and lettuce and top everything with my punchy Carrot Ginger Dressing (page 112), which brings brightness and warmth to every bite. The salad itself is endlessly flexible—add shredded cabbage, avocado, radish, or even fruit like mango or citrus segments, depending on what's in season. The dressing pulls it all together, and the edamame gives it just enough substance to feel like more than just a side. That said, it still works beautifully as a side, especially paired with something rich like my Tofu Katsu Makhani (page 33).

⅓ cup (45 g) frozen shelled edamame
4 to 6 ounces (113 to 170 g) crisp lettuce, roughly chopped or torn
¼ cup (15 g) microgreens, optional
1 medium carrot, cut into matchsticks
1 small Persian cucumber, sliced
⅓ cup (80 ml) Carrot Ginger Dressing (page 112), or to taste

1. Bring about 3 cups (720 ml) water to a boil in a large saucepan. Add the edamame and cook until tender, 3 to 5 minutes. Drain and rinse under cold water.
2. Transfer the edamame to a large bowl and toss it together with the lettuce, microgreens (if using), carrots, and cucumber. Transfer to a serving dish, if desired.
3. Spoon the Carrot Ginger Dressing over the salad and serve immediately.

# TOFU LETTUCE WRAP SALAD

## *with Carrot Ginger Dressing*

Serves 4 as a light main or side

I'm not embarrassed to admit that my first time having a tofu lettuce wrap was at P.F. Chang's, one of my family's go-to spots for Asian American food in the early 2000s. While the popular restaurant chain is sometimes criticized for being "too Americanized," especially by those of us in the Asian American community, I've come to appreciate how it introduced a wider audience—including my own family—to flavors we might not have otherwise explored. In fact, it sparked our curiosity and eventually led us to seek out local Asian-owned restaurants and expand our palates even more.

This recipe is inspired by those early lettuce wrap memories. My Carrot Ginger Dressing (page 112) brings a brightness to the savory tofu filling, while crunchy water chestnuts add that satisfying texture I remember loving in the restaurant version. I like to use green leaf lettuce for crispness or butter lettuce for a softer bite—though any lettuce you have on hand will work just fine. I serve this as a large salad with all the components layered on a large platter, but you can also serve with the individual components separated and then made into individual lettuce wraps or cups.

1 tablespoon neutral oil
1 large shallot or small red onion, diced (about ½ cup/75 g)
8 scallions, thinly sliced
6 garlic cloves, minced (about 2 tablespoons)
1½ teaspoons minced ginger
One 14-ounce (397 g) block extra firm tofu, drained
One 8-ounce (227 g) can water chestnuts, drained and roughly chopped
1½ tablespoons soy sauce
1 tablespoon mirin, optional
1 tablespoon rice vinegar
1 teaspoon maple syrup or preferred sweetener, to taste
Freshly cracked black and/or white pepper, to taste
2 to 3 small heads lettuce (such as green leaf or butter leaf)
¼ medium red cabbage, thinly sliced
1 cup (240 ml) Carrot Ginger Dressing (page 112), or to taste

1. Heat the oil in a large skillet or wok over medium heat. Add the shallot, scallions, garlic, and ginger, and stir frequently with a wooden spoon until very fragrant and just starting to brown, 3 to 5 minutes.
2. Add the tofu and water chestnuts, and use a fork to mash the tofu into crumbles. Stir well to combine. Continue to cook, stirring occasionally, until most of the liquid has evaporated and the tofu starts to brown, about 10 minutes.
3. Add the soy sauce, mirin (if using), rice vinegar, maple syrup, and pepper, and stir frequently until the sauce thickens and starts to caramelize, 2 to 3 minutes. Remove from the heat.
4. To serve, evenly layer the lettuce onto a large platter. Top with the tofu, cabbage, and dressing and serve immediately.

# GARAM MASALA BALSAMIC VINAIGRETTE

Makes ½ cup (120 ml)

Here, the cozy, warm spices that make up garam masala—cinnamon, cardamom, and clove—add an unexpected but delightful twist to a classic balsamic vinaigrette. The rich tang of balsamic vinegar, the subtle heat of Dijon mustard, and the savory depth of garlic all come together beautifully with these fragrant spices. A touch of maple syrup rounds out the dressing, gently enhancing the natural sweetness hidden within the garam masala.

¼ cup (60 ml) olive oil
3 tablespoons balsamic vinegar, plus more to taste
1 tablespoon maple syrup, plus more to taste
1 tablespoon Dijon mustard
1 or 2 garlic cloves, minced (about 1½ teaspoons)
1½ teaspoons garam masala, plus more to taste
Salt

1. Place the oil, balsamic vinegar, maple syrup, mustard, garlic, and garam masala and ½ teaspoon salt in a small blender. Blend until smooth. Taste and adjust for salt, acid (balsamic vinegar), warmth (garam masala), and sweetness (maple syrup).
2. Serve as desired or store in an airtight container in the refrigerator for up to 5 days.

# CARROT, PISTACHIO, AND MINT SALAD

Serves 2 to 4 as a side

The humble carrot often flies under the radar, but it truly deserves the spotlight. Its natural sweetness and subtle earthiness make it incredibly versatile, yet it shines brightest when paired with flavors and textures that contrast and elevate it. In this recipe, the warm spices of my Garam Masala Balsamic Vinaigrette (page 119) perfectly complement the carrot's natural sweetness. To add a delightful crunch and a touch of richness to this salad, I toss in chopped pistachios, which provide a buttery texture and nutty flavor that make every bite interesting. A handful of fresh mint leaves adds a refreshing and herbaceous bite. Together, these elements transform simple carrots into a vibrant, multidimensional salad that's anything but ordinary—a perfect example of how humble ingredients, when combined thoughtfully, are much more than the sum of their parts.

2 to 3 large carrots
½ batch (60 ml) Garam Masala Balsamic Vinaigrette (page 119), or to taste
¼ cup (28 g) pistachios, chopped, plus more for serving
¼ cup (7 g) fresh mint leaves, roughly chopped or torn

1 Use a vegetable peeler to peel the carrots into thin ribbons. Toss them together with the Garam Masala Balsamic Vinaigrette, pistachios, and mint. Top with extra chopped pistachios and serve immediately.

# BEANS, GREENS, AND GRAINS SALAD

Serves 2 to 4 as a main

Combining beans, greens, and grains creates a perfectly balanced and hearty meal that keeps you full and energized for hours. Beans are a rich source of plant-based protein and fiber, which promote sustained fullness and steady energy release. The greens add a crisp contrast of texture and color, while the whole grains offer complex carbohydrates that round out the dish with a filling base.

This trio of ingredients delivers not only on nutrition but also on texture and flavor, making each bite fulfilling. It's the kind of meal that holds you over through busy workdays or replenishes your body after a long afternoon. Whether you prepare the Garam Masala Balsamic Vinaigrette (page 119) ahead of time or whip it up fresh, this dish comes together quickly and effortlessly.

- 1 cup (170 g) cooked beans (such as white beans, black beans, kidney beans, or a combination; see Note 1)
- 2 tablespoons Garam Masala Balsamic Vinaigrette (page 119), divided, plus more to taste
- 1 cup (185 g) cooked grains (such as farro, barley, or wild rice) or quinoa (see Note 2)
- 2 to 4 ounces (57 to 113 g) crisp lettuce or mixed leafy greens
- 1 small Persian cucumber, sliced

1. Mix the beans with 1 tablespoon Garam Masala Balsamic Vinaigrette in a small bowl.
2. Mix the grains with 1 tablespoon Garam Masala Balsamic Vinaigrette in another small bowl.
3. Arrange the beans, grains, greens, and cucumber on a large serving plate. Drizzle with more vinaigrette to taste and serve immediately.

NOTES

1 I like to use drained and rinsed canned beans here for ease of preparation.

2 Quinoa is technically a seed, not a grain.

# CREAMY FIVE SPICE SAUCE

Makes about 1 cup (240 ml)

Nuts and seeds have long been cherished staples in Chinese and Vietnamese cuisines, prized not only for their rich flavor but also for their ability to create luscious, creamy sauces that add depth, texture, and nuttiness to dishes like noodles and fresh spring rolls. While peanut- and sesame-based sauces and dressings are classics, you can expand your culinary repertoire by exploring other nut and seed butters—adding an unexpected twist to everyday dishes.

This sauce is enhanced by the warm, aromatic notes of five spice powder, which is a fragrant blend of spices such as star anise, cloves, cinnamon, fennel, and peppercorns that's characteristic of both Chinese and Vietnamese cuisines. This spice mix imparts a subtle sweetness that perfectly complements and elevates the creamy sauce. Versatile and full of character, this sauce is fantastic drizzled over noodles or rice bowls (pages 127 and 128).

½ cup (125 g) nut or seed butter (such as almond, peanut, mixed nut, or sunflower seed butter or tahini)
2 tablespoons maple syrup or preferred sweetener, or to taste
2 tablespoons rice vinegar, plus more to taste
2 tablespoons soy sauce, plus more to taste
1 tablespoon sriracha or similar chili sauce, plus more to taste
2 garlic cloves
1 teaspoon minced ginger
½ teaspoon five spice powder

1. Combine the nut butter, maple syrup, rice vinegar, soy sauce, sriracha, garlic, ginger, five spice powder, and ¼ cup (60 ml) water in a blender. Blend until smooth, adding more water, 1 tablespoon at a time, to achieve your desired consistency. Taste and adjust for salt (soy sauce), acid (rice vinegar), heat (sriracha), and sweetness (maple syrup).
2. Serve as desired or store in an airtight container in the refrigerator for up to 5 days.

# CREAMY FIVE SPICE NOODLES

Serves 2 as a main or 4 as a side

This noodle dish is incredibly easy to make, coming together in just minutes with minimal effort. Its versatility is one of its greatest strengths—you can enjoy it warm for a comforting meal or chilled for a refreshing option, making it perfect for packing as a quick work or school lunch. The base is delicious on its own, but feel free to customize by adding your favorite vegetables or proteins like tofu or tempeh to make it a heartier, more satiating meal. Whether you're meal prepping or throwing something together at the last minute, this dish adapts easily to whatever you have on hand or whatever you're craving.

3 to 4 ounces (85 to 113 g) dry buckwheat noodles
3.5 ounces (100 g) sugar snap peas, thinly sliced (about 1 cup)
1 medium carrot, cut into thin matchsticks
⅓ batch (80 ml) Creamy Five Spice Sauce (page 124), or to taste

**FOR SERVING**

Sliced scallions, optional
Toasted sesame seeds, optional

1. Bring a large pot of water to a boil. Boil the noodles for 4 minutes (or according to the package instructions) and then drain and rinse with cold water in a colander to cool.
2. Transfer to a large bowl. Use tongs to toss the noodles with the peas, carrots, and Creamy Five Spice Sauce. Top with scallions and sesame seeds. Serve at room temperature or chilled.

# CREAMY FIVE SPICE RICE BOWL

Serves 2 as a main

This rice bowl offers a perfect balance of flavors, temperatures, and textures that keeps every bite exciting. The comforting warmth of the rice pairs beautifully with the cool, smooth silken tofu, crisp fresh vegetables, and tender cooked broccoli. Topped with my velvety Creamy Five Spice Sauce (page 124), the dish is bursting with fragrant, layered flavors. A sprinkle of scallions adds a fresh brightness, while a touch of chili crisp delivers a spicy punch, making this bowl a vibrant meal.

½ bunch kale, stems removed and chopped
1 teaspoon toasted sesame oil
1 teaspoon rice vinegar
Salt
1 cup (200 g) cooked brown rice, freshly cooked
One 16-ounce (454 g) container silken tofu, drained
1 cup (150 g) steamed broccoli florets
2 celery stalks, thinly sliced on the bias
½ medium English cucumber, thinly sliced
¼ batch (60 ml) Creamy Five Spice Sauce (page 124), or to taste
2 scallions, thinly sliced
1 tablespoon chili crisp (such as Fly By Jing), or to taste
2 teaspoons white or black sesame seeds, for serving

1. Combine the kale, oil, and rice vinegar and a pinch of salt in a large bowl. Massage with clean fingers for a few minutes until wilted, 2 to 3 minutes.
2. Divide the rice between two serving bowls. Scoop the tofu out of the container and divide between the bowls. Top with the kale, broccoli, celery, and cucumber.
3. Top with the Creamy Five Spice Sauce, scallions, chili crisp, and sesame seeds, and serve immediately.

# LEMONY CORIANDER AND FENNEL TOFU "RICOTTA"

Makes about 2½ cups (625 g)

Tofu is a great plant-based alternative to ricotta thanks to its naturally soft, slightly crumbly texture and its ability to soak up flavor like a sponge. It acts as a blank canvas, taking on the flavors you give it. To make this "ricotta," I blend in a handful of cashews for creaminess, though you can skip them and still end up with a delicious result. The lemon juice is tangy and bright, and the coriander and fennel add a subtle citrusy flavor. This tofu ricotta is versatile enough for pasta dishes, heirloom tomato salads, or lasagna.

½ cup (70 g) unroasted, unsalted cashews
3 tablespoons lemon juice (from about 1½ lemons), plus more to taste
Zest of 1 lemon (about 1 teaspoon)
2 tablespoons nutritional yeast (see Note)
1 tablespoon white miso
1 garlic clove
Salt
One 14-ounce (397 g) block firm tofu, drained
2 teaspoons coriander seeds
1½ teaspoons fennel seeds
2 tablespoons olive oil

1 Combine the cashews, lemon juice and zest, nutritional yeast, miso, garlic, ¾ teaspoon salt, and ⅓ cup (80 ml) water in a high-speed blender. Blend until very smooth.

2 Mash the tofu with a fork to form fine, even crumbles and then stir in the blended cashew mixture.

3 Gently crush the coriander seeds and fennel seeds with a mortar and pestle.

4 Heat the oil in a small saucepan over medium heat. Add the seeds and toast until fragrant and starting to brown, about 1 minute. Pour the oil over the "ricotta" and stir well to combine. Taste and adjust for salt and acid (lemon juice).

5 Serve as desired or store in an airtight container in the refrigerator for up to 5 days.

**NOTE**

Nutritional yeast is *not* the same as yeast used for baking. It is an inactive yeast that is often used in vegan cooking to add a cheesy flavor. Many nutritional yeast brands are also fortified with B vitamins, providing an added nutrient boost. If you can't find it, simply omit.

# GRILLED SQUASH AND EGGPLANT

## *with Lemony Tofu "Ricotta" and Chili Crisp Panko*

Serves 2 as a main or 4 as a side

I've always loved a good vegetable cutlet—crispy, golden, and incredibly satisfying. As much as I enjoy these cutlets in dishes like eggplant Parmesan, I don't always have the time (or patience) for the breading and frying that traditional recipes require. This recipe was born out of that craving for comfort with a desire for something quicker and easier.

Here, I grill slices of summer squash and eggplant until tender and then top them with a crisp, golden chili crisp panko that delivers all the crunch and flavor of a classic cutlet with a fraction of the effort. If you don't have a grill pan, you can sear the veg in a skillet. Serve this as a main or as a hearty vegetable side.

- 1 to 2 tablespoons olive oil
- 1 large or 2 small yellow squash, sliced
- 1 large or 2 small zucchini, sliced
- 1 Japanese eggplant or 4 to 6 baby eggplants, sliced
- Salt
- ½ cup (40 g) panko breadcrumbs
- 1 tablespoon chili crisp (such as Fly By Jing)
- 1 tablespoon sesame seeds
- ½ batch Lemony Coriander and Fennel Tofu "Ricotta" (page 131)
- 1 to 2 scallions, thinly sliced, for serving

1. Place a grill pan over medium-high heat. Brush a thin layer of oil onto both sides of the yellow squash, zucchini, and eggplant slices. Working in batches, place the squash, zucchini, and eggplant slices in an even layer on the grill pan. Cook until grill marks form and then flip and cook again, about 3 minutes per side. Sprinkle with salt to taste and set aside.
2. Heat a medium skillet over medium heat. Add the panko and toast, stirring frequently, until lightly browned, about 3 minutes. Add the chili crisp, sesame seeds, and ¼ teaspoon salt, and stir well to combine. Remove from the heat.
3. Spread a generous layer of the Lemony Coriander and Fennel Tofu "Ricotta" onto a large serving plate. Arrange the grilled squash and eggplant on top. Top with the panko and scallions and serve immediately.

# LEMONY TOFU "RICOTTA" STUFFED SHELLS

Serves 6 as a main

I started making baked pasta dishes like stuffed pasta shells in college. They were reliable, no-fuss meals that kept me fed for days. My early versions weren't anything fancy—they were made with dry pasta and jarred marinara—just classic comfort food that checked all the boxes. Over time, though, I began craving more flavor and a plant-based twist that felt a little more special.

This updated version of stuffed shells is still just as easy to make, but it's elevated by my Lemony Coriander and Fennel Tofu "Ricotta" (page 131), which adds a bright, herby flavor. The tofu base mimics the texture of traditional ricotta, while the lemon, coriander, and fennel flavors cut through the richness. It's a nostalgic favorite, made new with just a few upgrades.

I call for Tikka Masala Sauce (page 37) here, but you can easily use your favorite jarred tomato sauce or homemade marinara. You can also experiment with one of the other curries in this book, such as my Makhani Sauce (page 30), Spinach and Herb Saag (page 56), or Beet Korma (page 63).

25 to 30 dry jumbo pasta shells
½ cup (70 g) unroasted, unsalted cashews
¼ cup (15 g) nutritional yeast, optional (see Note)
2 tablespoons lemon juice (from about 1 lemon)
Salt
4 cups (960 ml) Tikka Masala Sauce (page 37) or sauce of choice (see Headnote), divided
1 batch Lemony Coriander and Fennel Tofu "Ricotta" (page 131)
Drizzle of olive oil, optional

## FOR SERVING

¼ cup (4 g) fresh cilantro or parsley leaves, roughly chopped
¼ cup (38 g) crispy fried onions, optional
Crushed red pepper flakes, to taste, optional

1. Bring a large pot of water to a boil and cook the pasta shells until al dente, according to the package instructions.
2. Preheat the oven to 375°F (190°C).
3. Combine the cashews, nutritional yeast, lemon juice, ½ teaspoon salt, and ⅓ cup (80 ml) water in a high-speed blender and blend until very smooth.
4. Spread about 2 cups (480 ml) Tikka Masala Sauce into a 9 × 13-inch (23 × 33 cm) baking dish.
5. Fill each pasta shell with about 1 tablespoon Lemony Coriander and Fennel Tofu "Ricotta" and place in the baking dish in an even layer.
6. Top with the remaining 2 cups (480 ml) Tikka Masala Sauce and drizzle with the blended cashew mixture. Drizzle with olive oil, if using.
7. Cover the baking dish with foil and bake for 20 minutes, or until the sauce is bubbling and the pasta is fully heated through. Remove the foil and broil for 1 to 2 minutes, if desired, to achieve browned crispy bits on top.
8. Top with the cilantro, fried onions, and red pepper flakes, if using, and serve immediately.

### NOTE

Nutritional yeast is *not* the same as yeast used for baking. It is an inactive yeast that is often used in vegan cooking to add a cheesy flavor. Many nutritional yeast brands are also fortified with B vitamins, providing an added nutrient boost. If you can't find it, simply omit.

# MANCHURIAN SAUCE

Makes 2 cups (480 ml)

Manchurian sauce is one of the fundamental sauces of Indo-Chinese cuisine—a beloved culinary tradition that emerged from the Chinese communities in Kolkata and has since become a staple across India and the world. This sauce captures everything people love about the cuisine: It's salty, tangy, spicy, a little sweet, and packed with umami. It's the flavor blueprint behind iconic dishes like gobi Manchurian (crispy cauliflower) and vegetable Manchurian (vegetable fritters).

One of the key ingredients in this version is ketchup. It might seem out of place at first, but it delivers sweetness, acidity, and an extra dose of umami. Whether you like ketchup or not, you won't taste it here—it simply disappears into the sauce. I also include a touch of MSG (monosodium glutamate) to further enhance the savoriness. MSG has long been misunderstood in the West, where fears about its safety have been largely fueled by misinformation and xenophobic attitudes toward Asian cuisines. In reality, MSG is a well-studied flavor enhancer that's safe and effective.

This sauce is endlessly adaptable: Spoon it over crispy tofu, toss it with stir fried vegetables, or use it as a dip for anything that needs a savory lift. Once you make it, you'll understand why it's considered the mother sauce of Indo-Chinese cooking.

3 tablespoons soy sauce, plus more to taste
2 tablespoons ketchup
1½ tablespoons maple syrup or preferred sweetener, or to taste
1 tablespoon cornstarch
1 tablespoon white vinegar, plus more to taste
Freshly cracked black pepper, to taste
¼ teaspoon MSG, optional
2 tablespoons neutral oil
1 jalapeño or preferred green chili, seeded for milder spice, minced
9 garlic cloves, minced (about 3 tablespoons)
4 scallions, minced
1 tablespoon minced ginger

1. Whisk together the soy sauce, ketchup, maple syrup, cornstarch, white vinegar, black pepper, MSG (if using), and 2 cups (480 ml) water in a small bowl until well combined.
2. Heat the oil in a medium saucepan over medium heat and add the jalapeño, garlic, scallions, and ginger. Stir frequently until the aromatics are very fragrant and starting to brown, about 5 minutes. Reduce the heat slightly to prevent burning, if needed.
3. Add the soy sauce mixture, bring to a gentle boil, and whisk until the cornstarch no longer appears cloudy and the mixture reduces to about 2 cups (480 ml), about 5 minutes.
4. Remove from the heat. Taste and adjust for salt (soy sauce), acid (white vinegar), and sweetness (maple syrup).
5. Serve as desired or store in an airtight container in the refrigerator for up to 5 days.

# VEGETABLE PANCAKES

## *with Manchurian Sauce*

Makes 2 large pancakes (serves 2 to 4)

This dish is a spin on vegetable Manchurian—a beloved Indo-Chinese dish of vegetable dumplings in a tangy and allium-forward Manchurian sauce. The traditional version requires finely chopping vegetables and deep frying the dumplings, but I wanted to make a version that was easier and more weeknight-friendly.

Enter vegetable pancakes inspired by Korean yachaejeon: crispy, savory vegetable pancakes dipped in a soy sauce–based dipping sauce. I learned to make these from my friend Joanne's (@thekoreanvegan) recipes. This version uses many of the same veggies you'd find in Manchurian dumplings without the deep frying. The result is a pancake that is crispy-edged, tender in the center, and ideal for soaking up my Manchurian Sauce (page 136).

¼ small green cabbage, thinly sliced (about 2 cups/175 g)
1 small red onion, thinly sliced (about 1 cup/150 g)
1 large carrot, cut into matchsticks (about 1 cup/80 g)
4 scallions, sliced
Salt
¼ cup plus 2 tablespoons (45 g) all-purpose flour, plus more as needed
2 tablespoons cornstarch
Freshly cracked black pepper, to taste
2 to 4 tablespoons olive oil, divided

### FOR SERVING

1 batch Manchurian Sauce (page 136)
2 scallions, thinly sliced
Chopped fresh cilantro leaves, to taste
Gochugaru or crushed red pepper flakes, to taste

1. Combine the cabbage, onions, carrots, and scallions and ¾ teaspoon salt in a large bowl, massaging the salt evenly into the vegetables with clean hands. Set aside for about 5 minutes, squeezing the vegetables every minute or so, until the vegetables release liquid and feel wet. You may see up to a few tablespoons of liquid accumulating at the bottom of the bowl; this will be used to form the pancake batter.
2. Stir in the flour, cornstarch, and black pepper to form a batter that lightly coats the vegetables, adding an additional tablespoon of flour at a time if the mixture is too watery. If it's too dry, add water 1 teaspoon at a time. It will look like there's barely enough batter to hold the vegetables together.
3. Heat a large nonstick skillet over medium heat. Add 1 to 2 tablespoons oil, followed by about half of the pancake mixture, spreading it thinly and evenly over the pan (7 to 8 inches/18 to 20 cm in diameter). Cook for about 5 minutes, flip, and cook for about 5 minutes further, until evenly browned on both sides. Lower the heat as needed to prevent burning. Transfer to a paper towel–lined plate and repeat with the remaining batter.
4. While the pancakes are cooking, warm the Manchurian Sauce in a medium saucepan over medium-low heat.
5. Slice the pancakes into bite-size squares and serve with the Manchurian Sauce as a dipping sauce or drizzled on top. Top with the scallions, cilantro, and gochugaru, and serve immediately.

# VEGETABLE WONTONS

## *with Manchurian Sauce*

Makes 40 to 50 wontons

Folded dumplings are a hallmark of many Asian cuisines. Examples include Chinese wontons, Japanese gyoza, and Korean mandu. So, these wontons are a natural fit to be served with my Indo-Chinese Manchurian Sauce (page 136). Folding dumplings at home can be time-consuming, but I find the process surprisingly meditative—a quiet, rhythmic task that invites you to slow down and be present. There's something almost therapeutic about filling and shaping each one by hand, and it's even better when you make them with others. Invite friends or family to join in, and suddenly what could feel like a chore turns into a joyful group activity—full of conversation, laughter, and a little bit of healthy competition over whose dumplings are the neatest.

1 tablespoon neutral oil
3 garlic cloves, minced (about 1 tablespoon)
3 scallions, minced
1 tablespoon minced ginger
½ medium green or purple cabbage, diced (about 3 cups/300 g)
2 to 3 medium carrots, diced (about 1 cup/140 g)
Salt
Freshly cracked black and white pepper, to taste
¼ teaspoon MSG, optional
1 cup (135 g) frozen shelled edamame
One 12-ounce (340 g) package vegan wonton wrappers

### FOR SERVING

1 batch Manchurian Sauce (page 136), or to taste
4 scallions, thinly sliced
1 teaspoon toasted white sesame seeds

#### TIP

These dumplings freeze beautifully. I like to make a big batch and stash them in the freezer for future meals. If you're making the wontons ahead, store them on a tray in an even layer in the refrigerator for up to 2 days or freeze on a parchment paper-lined baking sheet and then transfer to a food storage bag and store in the freezer for up to 3 months. When you're ready to cook, there's no need to thaw—just boil them straight from frozen, adding a few extra minutes to ensure they're fully cooked through.

1. Prepare the wonton filling: Heat the oil in a large skillet or wok over medium heat. Add the garlic, scallions, and ginger, and cook until fragrant and starting to brown, about 1 minute.
2. Add the cabbage, carrots, ½ teaspoon salt, black and white pepper, and MSG, if using. Cook, stirring occasionally, until the vegetables start to soften and brown, about 5 minutes. Lower the heat slightly if needed to prevent burning.
3. Add the edamame and cook, stirring occasionally, until fully heated through, about 5 minutes. Remove from the heat and transfer the vegetables to a bowl to cool slightly.
4. Transfer to a food processor and process to form a chunky paste. Season with more salt and black pepper to taste, but don't add too much, as the sauce will be well seasoned.
5. Fold the wontons: Place a damp kitchen towel or paper towel over the wonton wrappers to keep them moist. Have a small bowl of water on the side for sealing. Work with one wrapper at a time. With the point of the wrapper facing toward you, place 1½ to 2 teaspoons filling in the center, leaving at least ½ inch (1 cm) around the filling to prevent over-stuffing.
6. Using clean fingers, spread water on all four edges of the wrapper. Bring the bottom point up to the top point and tightly seal the two sides to form a triangle. Bring the bottom two edges together, moisten with water, and press together to form a wonton. Place onto a plate and repeat with the remaining wrappers and filling (see Tip if preparing ahead).
7. When ready to serve, warm the Manchurian Sauce in a medium saucepan over low heat.
8. Bring a large pot of water to a boil. Add about 10 wontons at a time, to avoid overcrowding the pot, and cook until the wontons rise to the top and are somewhat translucent, 3 to 5 minutes. Using a slotted spoon or spider strainer, transfer the wontons to a serving plate. Repeat to cook the remaining dumplings. Top with the Manchurian Sauce, scallions, and sesame seeds, and serve immediately.

# LEMON PEPPER GLAZE

Makes 1¼ cups (300 ml)

This vibrant, punchy glaze is built around one of the most widely used and accessible spices: peppercorns, which are native to the Malabar Coast of southwest India. Here, black peppercorns offer a spicy and almost fruity warmth, while white peppercorns provide a mellow earthiness. Lemon and fennel add brightness and a subtle floral lift, bringing out the aroma of the pepper. This is *not* the place for the preground black pepper that's been sitting at the back of your pantry for years—freshly cracked, high-quality whole peppercorns make all the difference here. Bonus points if they're sourced from India, where pepper is still grown with care.

1 teaspoon fennel seeds
1 teaspoon black peppercorns
½ teaspoon white peppercorns
¼ cup (60 ml) maple syrup, plus more to taste
3 tablespoons lemon juice (from about 1½ lemon), plus more to taste
1½ teaspoons lemon zest (from about 1½ lemons)
½ tablespoon cornstarch
¼ teaspoon ground turmeric
Salt
1 tablespoon olive oil
3 garlic cloves, minced (about 1 tablespoon)
2 teaspoons minced ginger

1. Crush the fennel seeds, black peppercorns, and white peppercorns with a mortar and pestle (or spice grinder) to form a coarse powder.
2. Whisk together the maple syrup, lemon juice and zest, cornstarch, turmeric, ½ teaspoon salt, and 1 cup (240 ml) water in a small bowl.
3. Heat the oil in a medium saucepan over medium heat. Add the garlic and ginger, and stir until fragrant and just starting to brown, about 3 minutes. Add the crushed spices, stir for a few seconds, and then pour the liquid mixture into the saucepan. Continue whisking over medium heat until a pourable glaze forms, about 3 minutes. Taste and adjust for salt, acid (lemon juice), and sweetness (maple syrup).
4. Serve as desired or store in an airtight container in the refrigerator for up to 5 days.

# LEMON PEPPER TOFU AND BROCCOLI

Serves 2 as a main

While broccoli and tofu might not sound like the most exciting meal, my Lemon Pepper Glaze (page 145) brings this humble and nourishing duo to new heights. The glaze provides a zingy and crave-worthy bite that ties everything together. Since the glaze comes together in a pinch, this is a versatile, weeknight-friendly recipe that delivers big flavor with minimal effort. Serve it over rice or grains or just on its own for a vibrant main. You can cook the broccoli a few different ways: Steam it, blanch it, or simply toss it into the pan with the tofu for a one-skillet meal. For faster, more efficient cooking, I like to cut the tofu into larger triangles—they sear beautifully, hold their shape, and cook quickly without drying out.

1 to 2 tablespoons olive oil
One 14-ounce (397 g) block extra firm tofu, drained and pressed for 30 minutes (see Tip), cut into bite-size cubes or larger triangles
1 batch Lemon Pepper Glaze (page 145)

**FOR SERVING**

2 scallions, thinly sliced, optional
1 large head broccoli, cut into bite-size florets and steamed (see Headnote)
2 cups (400 g) cooked rice

1. Heat the oil in a large nonstick pan over medium heat. Add the tofu pieces in an even layer and cook until evenly browned on all or most sides, about 3 minutes per side.
2. Add the Lemon Pepper Glaze and stir to coat the tofu pieces evenly. Continue to cook until the sauce is heated through and starts to thicken, 2 to 3 minutes.
3. Top with the scallions, if using, and serve hot with the broccoli and rice.

**TIP**

Use a tofu press for best results, but if you don't have one, you can place the tofu between two paper towels or clean kitchen towels. Place a flat plate or cutting board on top of the tofu and a few heavy cans (like beans) or books on top of the plate.

# GRILLED CORN

## *with Lemon Pepper Glaze*

Serves 4 as a side

When I was growing up in a mostly vegetarian household, our outdoor grill didn't see a lot of action—except when it came to corn. Grilled corn on the cob was a summer ritual: We ate it hot off the grill and finished the lightly charred kernels with a squeeze of lemon and a dusting of salt and chili powder. It was simple yet so satisfying. While we'd usually have the corncobs alongside veggie burgers, the corn was always what we'd look forward to the most.

This recipe is a tribute to those memories, dressed up just a bit with my Lemon Pepper Glaze (page 145). The glaze enhances the natural sweetness of peak-season corn while adding citrusy brightness and just the right amount of heat. It's the kind of dish that tastes like summer. You can also use this glaze to top other grilled vegetables such as zucchini, summer squash, carrots, bell peppers, and onions.

- 4 ears of corn, husks and silks removed
- ¼ cup (60 ml) Lemon Pepper Glaze (page 145), or to taste

1. Grill the corn on a grill or grill pan over medium-high heat (see Note). Turn it regularly while cooking to achieve an even charring of the corn kernels.
2. Transfer the corn to a serving plate and brush with the Lemon Pepper Glaze. Serve immediately.

**NOTE**
For very charred edges, cut the corncobs into quarters lengthwise with a large, sharp knife prior to grilling (as pictured).

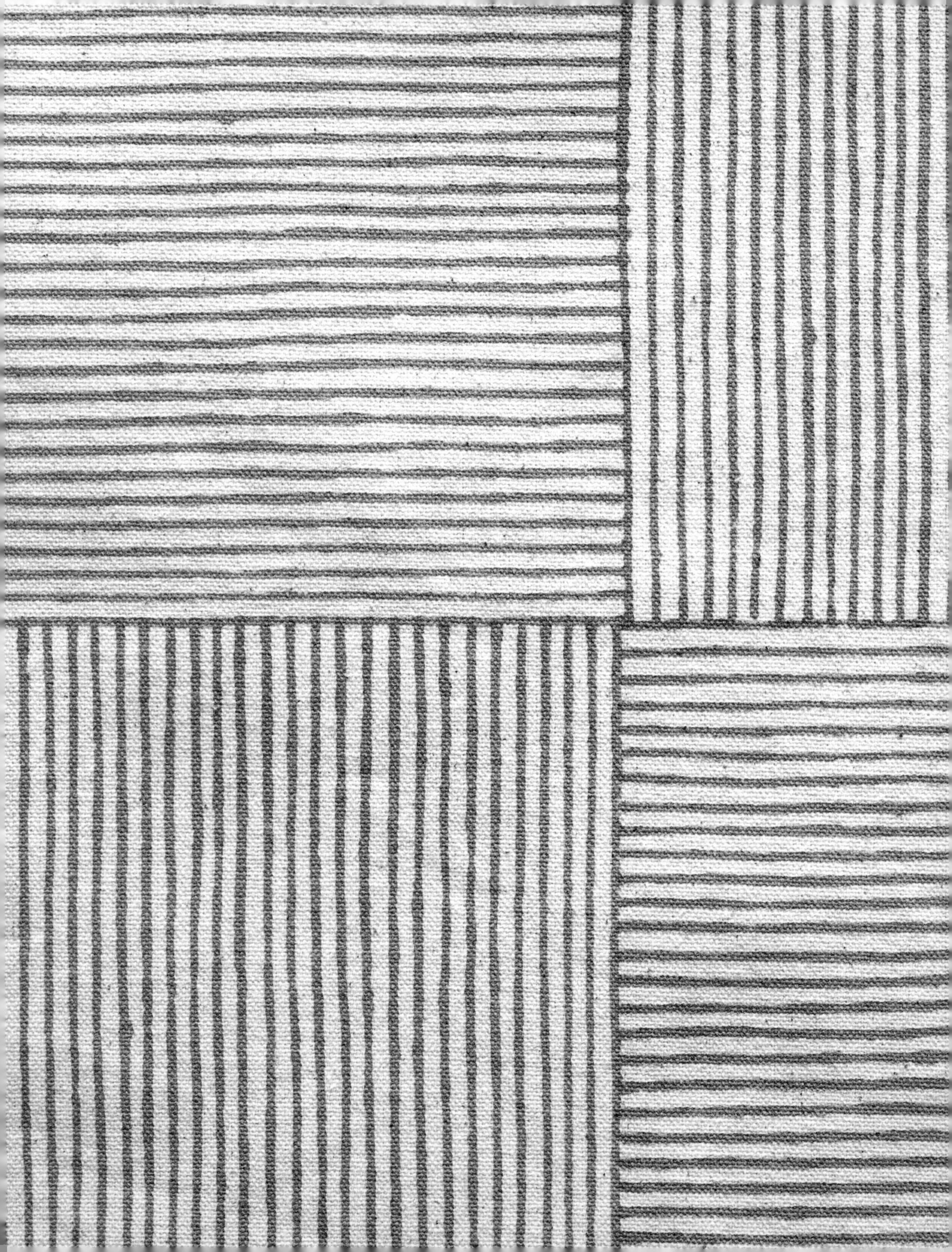

# HEARTY LEGUMES, GRAINS, AND STEWS

This chapter starts with Asia's mother grain: rice. It's the natural companion to any curry. The tender, mellow grains are perfectly suited to absorb rich flavors, but rice-based dishes can certainly stand on their own, too. Across India and beyond, rice is a staple ingredient that transcends borders, traditions, and cuisines. Whether it's steamed, stir fried, or made into porridge, it's the ultimate comfort food.

Pulses (such as lentils and legumes) play an equally essential role in South Asian cooking. These foods, like the daal that simmered on our stovetop many an evening during my childhood, are hearty and nourishing when served with other dishes or on their own. In South Asia, rice often takes on an even more nourishing role when paired with lentils, as in khichadi—a one-pot dish that's as soothing as it is sustaining.

This chapter focuses on these foundational ingredients—rice and pulses—and the many ways they can be prepared, enjoyed, and reimagined. Whether you're cooking a comforting bowl of tadka daal, a vibrant curry fried rice, or an herby, lemony lentil stew, these recipes are designed to stand alone as lead characters or pair effortlessly with other dishes as trusty sides. You'll find suggested pairings in my sample menus (see page 204), which can help you bring together balanced, flavorful meals with ease.

*Left to right, top to bottom: red lentils, French lentils, split yellow mung beans, brown jasmine rice, white sushi rice*

# FLUFFY BASMATI RICE

Makes about 3 cups (600 g)

You might be surprised—or even tempted to scoff—at the idea of boiling rice like pasta, but it's a method widely used in Indian restaurants, and it's how my mom has always made her basmati rice at home. By cooking the rice in a large pot of boiling water and then draining it, you get beautifully long, separate grains with a fluffy texture that's especially well suited for serving with curries or daals. This stovetop method offers a wonderfully simple and reliable alternative to rice cookers and pressure cookers, and it achieves perfect basmati rice without much guesswork. Once you try it, you may find it becomes your go-to technique for rice preparation.

1 cup (200 g) basmati rice
1 teaspoon neutral oil
½ teaspoon salt

1. Place the rice in a fine-mesh sieve and run cool tap water over it while swishing the grains between your fingers. Rinse until the water begins to run clear and then drain.
2. Place the rice, oil, and salt and 5 cups (1.2 L) water in a large pot or saucepan and bring to a boil over medium-high heat (see Tip). Reduce the heat slightly to maintain a gentle boil and cook until just barely tender, 6 to 8 minutes. Drain using a fine-mesh sieve.
3. Transfer to a serving bowl, and cover for 5 to 10 minutes to let the rice finish cooking. Fluff with a fork and serve immediately.

**TIP**
You can also add whole spices along with the rice while boiling for added flavor. Some of my favorites include a combination of star anise, ½ teaspoon cumin seeds, a cinnamon stick, 2 or 3 cloves, and/or 2 or 3 green cardamom pods.

# MUSHROOM RICE

Serves 4 to 6 as a main

This is my take on Japanese-style mushroom rice. It is one of my favorite rice dishes of all time because it is umami-forward (thanks to the miso, soy sauce, and mushrooms), and it has added depth of flavor from the star aromatics of Asian cuisine: onions, scallions, ginger, and garlic. For an additional boost of flavor and umami, I like to use a variety of different mushrooms, including beech, maitake, oyster, and king trumpet, but you can use whatever combination is accessible to you. It is best served right off the stove on a chilly day because the warmth and porridge-like consistency of the rice soothes the soul.

1½ cups (300 g) white sushi rice
2 tablespoons neutral oil, divided
16 ounces (454 g) mushrooms (see Headnote), cut into bite-size pieces
Salt
1 large yellow onion, diced (about 2 cups/300 g)
6 to 8 scallions, thinly sliced
6 garlic cloves, minced (about 2 tablespoons)
1 tablespoon minced ginger
1 tablespoon maple syrup or preferred sweetener
1 tablespoon mirin
1 tablespoon soy sauce, plus more to taste
2 tablespoons white miso

1. Place the rice in a fine-mesh sieve and run cool tap water over it while swishing the grains between your fingers. Rinse until the water begins to run clear and then drain. Transfer the rice to a medium bowl and add enough water to cover.
2. Heat 1 tablespoon oil in a large pot or Dutch oven over medium-high heat. Add the mushrooms in an even layer, and cook, stirring occasionally, until browned, about 10 minutes. Season with a pinch of salt and transfer the mushrooms to a medium bowl or plate.
3. Heat the remaining 1 tablespoon oil in the same large pot or Dutch oven over medium-high heat. Add the onions and a pinch of salt, and stir frequently with a wooden spoon until translucent and starting to brown, about 6 minutes. Lower the heat slightly, add the scallions, garlic, and ginger, and cook, stirring occasionally, until fragrant, about 1 minute. Add about two-thirds of the mushrooms, and stir to combine.
4. Drain the rice and add it to the pot along with the maple syrup, mirin, soy sauce, and 5½ cups (1.3 L) water. Stir and bring to a gentle simmer. Reduce the heat to low to maintain the gentle simmer, cover partially, and cook, stirring occasionally, until the rice is tender and most of the liquid has been absorbed, about 30 minutes. Check more frequently in the last 10 minutes of cooking to ensure the rice does not stick and burn on the bottom of the pot. Remove from the heat and stir in the miso until well incorporated. Taste and adjust for salt or soy sauce.
5. Transfer to serving bowls, top with the reserved mushrooms and serve immediately.

# FIERY BEAN AND VEGETABLE SOUP

Serves 4 as a main

This soup is inspired by rasam, a tangy, spicy, and comforting South Indian soup, and Korean chigae (stew) which is similarly tangy and spicy. The tang in rasam often comes from tamarind and/or tomato (I've used both here), and the spice and depth of flavor comes from rasam powder, a blend of lentils, chili, and spices like cumin and coriander. I make an abbreviated version of this powder here (you can omit the chana daal and fenugreek seeds if you don't have them), and I add gochugaru (Korean red chili; see page 17) to this soup for heat, but feel free to sub in any other type of chili to taste. Vegetables and beans make this soup a more complete meal, almost like a minestrone. Feel free to add pasta or serve with rice, too!

### SPICE POWDER

1 tablespoon chana daal (see Note 1)
1 tablespoon coriander seeds
1½ teaspoons cumin seeds
½ teaspoon black peppercorns
¼ teaspoon fenugreek seeds

### SOUP

1 tablespoon neutral oil
2 teaspoons gochugaru
1 medium red bell pepper, diced
1 medium carrot, diced
1 small red onion, diced
1 medium Yukon gold potato, peeled if desired, diced
Salt
3 garlic cloves, minced (about 1 tablespoon)
4 cups (960 ml) low-sodium vegetable broth
One 16-ounce (454 g) can kidney beans, drained and rinsed
1 medium zucchini, diced
1 medium plum tomato, diced
½ teaspoon tamarind concentrate or lime juice, plus more to taste

### TADKA

1 tablespoon neutral oil
½ teaspoon black mustard seeds
15 fresh curry leaves, thinly sliced
Pinch of asafetida
1 teaspoon gochugaru
¼ teaspoon ground turmeric

1 Make the spice powder: Heat the chana daal, coriander seeds, cumin seeds, peppercorns, and fenugreek seeds in a small skillet over medium heat, stirring frequently, until fragrant and just starting to brown, 3 to 5 minutes. Transfer to a bowl to cool and then blend in a spice grinder to form a powder (see Note 1).

2 Make the soup: Heat the oil in a large pot over medium heat. Add the gochugaru and stir, taking caution not to burn, until fragrant and deepening in color, less than 30 seconds. Add the bell peppers, carrots, onions, and potatoes and ½ teaspoon salt, and cook, stirring occasionally, until the vegetables start to brown and become tender, about 5 minutes.

3 Add the garlic and stir until fragrant, a few seconds. Add the broth, beans, zucchini, and tomato, and prepared spice powder, and stir well to combine. Simmer until all the vegetables are fully tender, stirring occasionally, about 15 minutes. Remove from the heat and stir in the tamarind concentrate.

4 Make the tadka: Heat the oil in a small saucepan over medium heat. Add the mustard seeds and cook until the seeds begin to pop, about 30 seconds. Add the curry leaves and asafetida and cook until the spluttering subsides, about 30 seconds.

5 Swirl in the gochugaru and turmeric and pour the mixture over the hot soup. Stir to combine. Season generously with salt to taste and add more tamarind concentrate to taste for acidity. Serve immediately (see Note 2).

### NOTES

1 Chana daal, also known as split Bengal gram, are husked and split brown chickpeas. They can be found at Indian grocers or online. If you don't have a spice grinder, you can use a mortar and pestle, but I would then recommend skipping the chana daal, since the daal can be difficult to grind to a powder even with a heavy mortar and pestle.

2 The soup thickens upon standing, so if you're making this ahead, add more water as needed to maintain a soupy consistency.

# FALL DAAL

Serves 4 to 6 as a main

Daal is an everyday lentil stew, and I like to use split red lentils to make this recipe even more everyday-friendly, since other lentils, such as toor daal (split pigeon peas) and whole moong daal (mung beans), can take longer to cook or are better made in a pressure cooker. Daal is usually topped with tadka (see page 20), a spiced oil that infuses the stew with tons of flavor. While many North Indian versions of tadka daal are served plain, without vegetables (unlike South Indian sambar, which is packed with veggies), I like to add butternut and honeynut squash to lighten up the daal and add a pleasant sweetness. Take this as an invitation to welcome other squash or root vegetables, such as beets or carrots, to your tadka daal party.

1 cup (190 g) red lentils
1 tablespoon olive oil
1 large yellow onion, diced (about 2 cups/300 g)
Salt
1 teaspoon cumin seeds
6 garlic cloves, minced (about 2 tablespoons)
1 teaspoon minced ginger
Pinch of asafetida, optional
1 teaspoon ground coriander
½ teaspoon ground turmeric
4 cups (550 g) peeled and diced hard-rind squash (such as butternut squash, honeynut squash, or a combination)
½ teaspoon garam masala, plus more to taste

### TADKA

1 tablespoon neutral oil
½ teaspoon black mustard seeds, optional
¼ teaspoon cumin seeds, optional
15 fresh curry leaves, thinly sliced
¼ teaspoon ground red chili, plus more to taste

### FOR SERVING, OPTIONAL

2 to 3 tablespoons chopped fresh cilantro leaves
Cooked brown or white rice

1. Place the lentils in a fine-mesh sieve and run under cool tap water while swishing the legumes between your fingers. Rinse until the water begins to run clear and then drain. Transfer the lentils to a medium bowl and add enough water to cover.
2. Heat the oil in a large pot or Dutch oven over medium heat. Add the onions and ½ teaspoon salt, and cook, stirring frequently with a wooden spoon, until translucent and evenly browned, about 8 minutes. Reduce the heat slightly if needed to prevent the onions from burning.
3. Add the cumin seeds and stir until fragrant and lightly browned, about 30 seconds.
4. Reduce the heat to medium-low. Add the garlic, ginger, and asafetida, if using, and stir until fragrant and starting to brown, about 2 minutes.
5. Add the coriander and turmeric, and stir until they are well combined and the turmeric deepens in color, about 30 seconds. Add 6 cups (1.4 L) water and stir well to combine.
6. Drain the lentils and add them to the pot along with the squash and ¾ teaspoon salt. Stir well to combine. Bring to a boil and then reduce the heat to low.
7. Simmer, uncovered, stirring occasionally, until the lentils and squash are fully tender and easily mashed with the back of a spoon, about 20 minutes. If foam accumulates on the surface of the liquid while cooking, skim and discard it.
8. Stir in the garam masala and remove from the heat. Use an immersion blender to blend until smooth.
9. Make the tadka: Heat the oil in a small saucepan over medium heat. Add mustard seeds and cumin seeds, if using, and cook until the mustard seeds begin to pop and the cumin seeds begin to brown, about 30 seconds. Add curry leaves and cook until crisp and the spluttering starts to subside, less than 1 minute.
10. Remove from the heat, swirl in the chili, and pour the mixture on top of the daal. Season generously with more salt to taste. Taste and adjust for warmth (garam masala) and heat (chili). Top with chopped cilantro, if using, and serve hot on its own or with rice.

# FRENCH LENTILS
## *with Lemon Rosemary Tadka*

Serves 4 as a main

I love keeping potted rosemary plants out on my patio in the warmer months—they're easy to grow, and they fill the air with their distinctive aroma. Combining rosemary with lemon zest and cumin in a tadka (see page 20) adds a wonderful citrusy and herbaceous note that beautifully perfumes the French lentils. While French lentils are more common in Western stews and salads, they aren't traditionally among the many varieties of pulses used in Indian cooking, simply because they are not traditionally grown in India. Their tender texture, subtle peppery and earthy flavor, and accessibility in many Western grocery stores make this dish especially inviting and approachable. It's a fantastic way to introduce Indian-inspired flavors and cooking techniques to anyone looking for something fresh, familiar, and hearty.

1 cup (200 g) whole French (Puy) lentils
2 tablespoons olive oil
1 large red onion, diced (about 2 cups/300 g)
Salt
1 teaspoon cumin seeds
1 jalapeño (or preferred green chili), seeded for milder spice, minced
6 garlic cloves, minced (about 2 tablespoons)
1 tablespoon minced ginger
½ teaspoon ground turmeric
1 fresh rosemary sprig (about 6 inches/15 cm long)
Freshly cracked black pepper, to taste
1½ teaspoons lemon juice (from about ½ small lemon), plus more to taste

### TADKA

2 tablespoons olive oil
½ teaspoon cumin seeds
Zest of 1 lemon (about 1 teaspoon)
1 teaspoon roughly chopped fresh rosemary leaves
¼ teaspoon ground turmeric
Pinch of asafetida
Fluffy Basmati Rice (page 154), optional, for serving

1. Place the lentils in a fine-mesh sieve and run under cool tap water while swishing the legumes between your fingers. Rinse until the water begins to run clear and then drain. Transfer the lentils to a medium bowl and add enough water to cover.
2. Heat the oil in a large pot or Dutch oven over medium heat. Add the onions and ½ teaspoon salt, and cook, stirring frequently with a wooden spoon, until translucent and evenly browned, about 8 minutes. Reduce the heat slightly if needed to prevent the onions from burning.
3. Add the cumin seeds and stir until fragrant and lightly browned, about 30 seconds. Add the jalapeño, garlic, and ginger, and stir until fragrant and starting to brown, about 2 minutes.
4. Stir in the turmeric until well combined and deepened in color, about 30 seconds. Add 5 cups (1.2 L) water and stir well to combine.
5. Drain the lentils and add them to the pot along with the rosemary sprig, the black pepper, and ½ teaspoon salt. Stir well to combine. Bring to a boil and then reduce the heat to low. Simmer, partially covered, stirring occasionally, for 20 to 25 minutes, until the lentils are brothy and fully tender (see Tip). Remove from the heat and stir in the lemon juice.
6. Make the tadka: Heat the oil in a small saucepan over medium heat. Add the cumin seeds and cook until fragrant and just starting to brown, a few seconds. Add the lemon zest, rosemary leaves, turmeric, and asafetida and cook until fragrant, about 30 seconds.
7. Remove from the heat and pour over the lentils. Taste and adjust for salt and acid (lemon juice). Serve hot on its own or with rice.

### TIP

If your lentils are on the older side, they may require more water and time to cook. Simply add ½ to 1 cup (120 to 240 ml) more water as needed and continue to simmer until tender.

# SUSHI RICE KHICHADI

Serves 4 as a main

Khichadi is a beloved comfort food across India, often regarded as the ultimate nourishing dish. Traditionally made by slow-cooking rice and lentils together, and prized for its simplicity and versatility, it's served both as everyday home food and in times of celebration or healing. Each region and household has its own take, making khichadi a true culinary expression of Indian culture and tradition.

This recipe came to me as a happy surprise when I ran out of my usual basmati rice and had only half a cup of sushi rice left in the pantry. The sushi rice held up beautifully through the longer cooking process, and the tender, starchy grains combined well with the split red lentils to create a lovely creamy consistency.

My mom often made khichadi when I was a child—always with love and care, sometimes improvising with whatever grains were on hand. This dish is a nod to her resourcefulness and warmth. It has quickly become a favorite in my kitchen, reminding me that sometimes the best recipes come from happy accidents and family memories.

¾ cup (150 g) red lentils
¾ cup (150 g) white sushi rice
1 tablespoon olive oil
1 large yellow onion, diced (about 2 cups/300 g)
Salt
6 garlic cloves, minced (about 2 tablespoons)
1 tablespoon minced ginger
½ teaspoon ground turmeric
½ teaspoon garam masala

### TADKA

1 tablespoon neutral oil
½ teaspoon cumin seeds
½ teaspoon black mustard seeds
15 fresh curry leaves, torn or thinly sliced
Pinch of asafetida
¼ teaspoon ground turmeric

#### NOTE

If you prefer, you can add more heat in the form of a green chili (minced) along with the garlic and ginger or in the form of ground red chili in the tadka (swirled in along with the turmeric), but it tastes just as great without.

1. Place the lentils and rice in a fine-mesh sieve and run under cool tap water while swishing the grains and legumes between your fingers. Rinse until the water begins to run clear and then drain. Transfer the lentils and rice to a medium bowl and add enough water to cover.
2. Heat the oil in a large pot or Dutch oven over medium heat. Add the onions and ½ teaspoon salt, and cook, stirring frequently with a wooden spoon, until translucent and evenly browned, about 8 minutes. Reduce the heat slightly if needed to prevent the onions from burning.
3. Reduce the heat to medium-low. Add the garlic, ginger, and turmeric (see Note), and stir until fragrant, about 2 minutes. Add 6 cups (1.4 L) water and stir well to combine.
4. Drain the lentils and rice and add them to the pot along with ½ teaspoon salt. Stir well to combine. Bring to a boil and then reduce the heat to low.
5. Simmer, partially covered, stirring occasionally, until the lentils and rice are fully tender and easily mashed with the back of a spoon, 25 to 30 minutes. If foam accumulates on the surface of the liquid while cooking, skim and discard it. Add water if needed to maintain a creamy consistency.
6. Stir in the garam masala and remove from the heat.
7. Make the tadka: Heat the oil in a small saucepan over medium heat. Add the cumin seeds and mustard seeds and cook until the mustard seeds begin to pop, about 30 seconds. Add the curry leaves and asafetida and cook until the spluttering subsides, about 30 seconds.
8. Swirl in the turmeric and pour over the khichadi. Taste and adjust for salt. Serve immediately.

# SPRING KHICHADI

Serves 4 as a main

This springtime twist on my Sushi Rice Khichadi (page 165) bursts with vibrant green hues from fresh spinach and mint, complemented by the bright, crisp flavors of asparagus and radish. It's a celebration of the season's freshest produce, which brings lightness and freshness to the comforting khichadi base. Feel free to customize it with other vegetables—chopped carrots or golden beets can be added alongside or in place of the asparagus stems, and frozen green peas make a perfect addition in the last 5 minutes of cooking. This adaptable recipe invites you to make the most of spring's bounty in every nourishing bite.

¾ cup (165 g) split yellow moong daal (split yellow mung beans) or red lentils
¾ cup (150 g) white sushi rice
1 small bunch asparagus
2 tablespoons olive oil, divided
1 small red onion, finely diced (about 1 cup/150 g)
Salt
½ teaspoon cumin seeds
½ teaspoon fennel seeds
Pinch of asafetida
1 green chili (such as jalapeño), seeded for milder spice, minced
3 garlic cloves, minced (about 1 tablespoon)
1 tablespoon minced ginger
¼ teaspoon ground turmeric
2 to 3 ounces (57 to 85 g) baby spinach
¼ cup (about 7 g) packed fresh mint leaves
1 teaspoon lime juice (from about ½ small lime), plus more to taste
½ teaspoon garam masala
3 to 4 small red, pink, and/or purple radishes, thinly sliced, for serving

## TADKA

2 tablespoons neutral oil
½ teaspoon cumin seeds
15 fresh curry leaves, thinly sliced
Pinch of asafetida
½ teaspoon gochugaru or ground red chili, or to taste
¼ teaspoon ground turmeric

1 Place the lentils and rice in a fine-mesh sieve and run under cool tap water while swishing the grains and legumes between your fingers. Rinse until the water begins to run clear and then drain. Transfer the lentils and rice to a medium bowl and add enough water to cover.

2 Trim the asparagus and discard the woody bottoms. Cut off the top 3 inches (7.5 cm) of the asparagus, and set aside for serving. Thinly slice the remaining asparagus stems.

3 Heat 1 tablespoon oil in a large pot or Dutch oven over medium heat. Add the sliced asparagus, onions, and ½ teaspoon salt, and cook, stirring frequently with a wooden spoon, until the onions are translucent and starting to brown and the asparagus is tender, about 8 minutes. Reduce the heat slightly if needed to prevent the vegetables from burning.

4 Add the cumin seeds, fennel seeds, and asafetida, and stir until fragrant and lightly browned, about 30 seconds. Reduce the heat to medium-low. Add the chili, garlic, ginger, and turmeric, and stir until fragrant, about 2 minutes. Add 6 cups (1.4 L) water and stir well to combine.

5 Drain the lentils and rice and add them to the pot along with ½ teaspoon salt. Stir well to combine. Bring to a boil and then reduce the heat to low. Simmer, partially covered, stirring occasionally, until the lentils and rice are fully tender and easily mashed with the back of a spoon, about 30 minutes. If foam accumulates on the surface of the liquid while cooking, skim and discard it.

6 While the khichadi is cooking, combine the spinach, mint, and lime juice and ¼ cup (60 ml) water in a blender. Blend until very smooth.

7 Heat the remaining 1 tablespoon oil in a medium skillet over medium heat. Add the asparagus tips and cook, stirring occasionally, until tender and starting to brown, about 5 minutes. Season with salt to taste and remove from the heat.

8 When the khichadi has finished cooking, stir in the blended spinach and the garam masala, and remove from the heat.

9 Make the tadka: Heat the oil in a small saucepan over medium heat. Add the cumin seeds and cook until fragrant and just starting to brown, about 30 seconds. Add the curry leaves and asafetida and cook until the spluttering subsides, about 30 seconds. Swirl in the gochugaru and turmeric. Taste and adjust for salt and acid (lime juice).

10 To serve, transfer the hot khichadi to a serving bowl or individual bowls. Top with cooked asparagus tips, sliced radishes, and tadka. Serve immediately.

# HOMESTYLE INDIAN FRIED RICE

Serves 4 as a side

Vagharela bhaat is a beloved Gujarati way to transform leftover rice into a fragrant, flavorful meal—and this is my take on it. There's no single "right" way to prepare it; every family has their own version. This particular method comes from my mom, whose cooking mantra is simple: The more curry leaves you add, the better the dish tastes. To capture their vibrant, citrusy aroma, I like to thinly slice the curry leaves so their flavor infuses every bite.

While basmati rice is traditional here, feel free to swap in other cooked grains like barley, farro, or quinoa (technically a seed)—or even torn leftover roti or paratha (whole wheat flatbreads)—to make the dish your own. It's a wonderfully flexible recipe that celebrates both resourcefulness and bold, fresh flavors.

2 tablespoons olive oil
1 teaspoon cumin seeds
½ teaspoon black mustard seeds
15 to 20 fresh curry leaves, thinly sliced
¼ teaspoon asafetida
3 cups (600 g) Fluffy Basmati Rice (page 154)
1 teaspoon cane sugar or preferred sweetener, or to taste
¼ teaspoon ground red chili, plus more to taste
¼ teaspoon ground turmeric
Salt
1 teaspoon lime juice (from about ½ small lime), plus more to taste

1. Heat the oil in a large nonstick pan over medium heat. Add the cumin seeds and mustard seeds and cook until the mustard seeds begin to pop, about 30 seconds. Add the curry leaves and asafetida, and cook until the spluttering subsides, about 30 seconds.
2. Add the rice, sugar, chili, and turmeric and ½ teaspoon salt. Stir well to combine and cook until fully heated through, about 5 minutes.
3. Stir in the lime juice and remove from the heat. Taste and adjust for salt, acid (lime juice), sweetness (sugar), and heat (chili). Serve immediately.

# CURRY FRIED RICE

Serves 4 as a main

Curry fried rice is a staple on many Thai restaurant menus. It's usually made with curry powder that is deeply aromatic from spices such as citrusy coriander, earthy cumin, and sweet cardamom and cinnamon. It also has a characteristically yellow color from the turmeric in the curry powder. This rice dish is one of our go-to orders at Thai restaurants—especially when testing out a new restaurant, to see if it has the ideal flavor balance to keep us coming back.

While you won't typically find curry powder in traditional Indian home cooking, it brings together a mix of familiar spices in a way that works beautifully here. Think of this dish as a cousin to pineapple fried rice—bright, flavorful, and versatile. If you like, add some pineapple chunks to introduce a sweet, juicy contrast to the spicy warmth of the rice that elevates the dish even more.

This recipe is a great example of how Indian flavors can travel, adapt, and show up in unexpected, delicious ways. Plus, it's endlessly flexible—perfect for weeknights and ideal for using up leftover rice and whatever vegetables you've got in the fridge.

### SAUCE

2 tablespoons soy sauce, plus more to taste
1 tablespoon maple syrup
1 tablespoon rice vinegar
1 tablespoon sriracha, plus more to taste
1½ teaspoons curry powder, plus more to taste

### FRIED RICE

1 to 2 tablespoons neutral oil
1 to 2 shallots or 1 small red onion, thinly sliced
6 garlic cloves, minced (about 2 tablespoons)
1 tablespoon minced ginger
3 cups (300 to 350 g) vegetables (such as chopped broccoli, chopped cabbage, diced bell pepper, diced carrot, shelled edamame, and/or peas)
3 cups (600 g) cooked brown rice (see Note)

### FOR SERVING

Chopped cashews
Thinly sliced scallions

1. Make the sauce: Combine the soy sauce, maple syrup, rice vinegar, sriracha, and curry powder and 3 tablespoons water in a small bowl. Whisk to combine.
2. Make the fried rice: Heat the oil in a large pan or wok over medium-high heat. Add the shallots and stir until starting to brown, about 3 minutes. Add the garlic and ginger, and stir until fragrant, about 30 seconds. Add the vegetables and cook to desired doneness, 5 to 10 minutes. Lower the heat as needed to prevent burning.
3. Add the rice and the prepared sauce. Stir frequently and continue to cook until well combined and heated through.
4. Taste and adjust for salt (soy sauce), heat (sriracha), and warmth (curry powder). Top with the cashews and scallions and serve.

### NOTE

You can use short grain, basmati, or jasmine rice for this recipe. I like using brown rice in particular since it offers a tender chew that holds up to stir frying. It's best to use day-old refrigerated rice here for optimal texture.

# CURRY NOODLE STIR FRY

Serves 2 as a main or 4 as a side

Like my Curry Fried Rice (page 170), these noodles are another flavorful and approachable way to cook with curry powder. This is my take on Singapore noodles, which uses tofu in place of the traditional proteins like shrimp, pork, and scrambled eggs. Despite the name, Singapore noodles don't actually hail from Singapore. The dish is widely believed to have been created by Cantonese chefs in Hong Kong, who adapted it as a clever and delicious way to use curry powder—an ingredient introduced to the region through British colonial influence.

This dish exemplifies how culinary traditions evolve: a colonial import reimagined through Cantonese technique, resulting in something entirely new and wildly craveable. The curry powder lends a warm, aromatic backbone that pairs beautifully with the stir fried noodles and crisp-tender vegetables. I also love this recipe as a fridge-cleanout meal—it's adaptable and a great way to use up odds and ends of whatever vegetables you have on hand. It's quick and packed with flavor—proof that a pantry staple like curry powder still has plenty of exciting places to go.

4 ounces (113 g) dry rice vermicelli noodles
7 ounces (198 g) extra firm tofu, drained
2 tablespoons neutral oil, divided
2½ teaspoons curry powder, divided, plus more to taste
Salt
Freshly cracked white pepper, to taste
6 garlic cloves, minced (about 2 tablespoons)
6 scallions, thinly sliced, 1 to 2 tablespoons greens reserved for serving
1½ teaspoons minced ginger
2 medium carrots, cut into matchsticks
1 small red bell pepper, thinly sliced
1 small red onion, thinly sliced
¼ small green cabbage, thinly sliced
1 tablespoon soy sauce
2 teaspoons rice vinegar or lime juice, plus more to taste
1 teaspoon cane sugar or preferred sweetener, or to taste

### FOR SERVING

2 scallions, thinly sliced
2 to 3 tablespoons roughly chopped fresh cilantro leaves

1. Bring a large pot of water to a boil. Add the noodles and remove from the heat. Allow the noodles to soften to a pliable consistency, 5 to 10 minutes. Rinse under cold water, drain, and set aside.
2. Mash the tofu with a fork in a small bowl to form even crumbles.
3. Heat 1 tablespoon oil in a large wok or pan over medium heat. Add the tofu and cook, stirring frequently until evenly light brown, about 5 minutes. Add ½ teaspoon curry powder, ¼ teaspoon salt, and white pepper to taste. Stir well to combine. Transfer the tofu to a bowl and set aside.
4. Heat the remaining 1 tablespoon oil in the same wok over medium-high heat. Add the garlic, scallions, and ginger, and stir until fragrant, about 30 seconds. Add the carrots, bell peppers, onions, and cabbage and ½ teaspoon salt, and cook, stirring frequently, until softened and starting to brown, about 6 minutes.
5. Add the remaining 2 teaspoons curry powder and stir well to combine. Add the cooked noodles, soy sauce, rice vinegar, and sugar, and stir well to combine. Cook until the noodles are tender, about 3 minutes. Add water, 1 to 2 tablespoons at a time, if the noodles become too dry, and reduce the heat as needed to prevent burning.
6. Taste and adjust for salt, acid (rice vinegar), and warmth (curry powder). Top with the sliced scallions and cilantro, and serve immediately.

# BREADS

There's something deeply comforting about tearing a warm piece of freshly made flatbread to scoop up a bite of rich, spiced curry. Breads like garlic naan and paratha may not be strictly essential to a curry meal, but they are undeniably special. They turn a bowl of curry into an incredibly satisfying experience.

That said, I'll be honest: When I'm cooking a curry on a busy weeknight, I'm not always up for making bread from scratch, too. And that's okay. These recipes aren't about pressure—they're about joy. Think of them as your weekend projects, to be made only when you have a bit more time to slow down and enjoy the process. Or, if you've prepped your curry the day before, you might find that making a fresh bread the next day is not only achievable but actually fun.

The three breads in this small but mighty chapter—Garlic Naan (page 178), Flaky Scallion Paratha (page 181), and Khichadi Paratha (page 182)—may be few in number, but they hold a lot of meaning. Each one draws on family traditions and memories: Naan was a restaurant favorite of mine as a child, always requested for special occasions; paratha reminds me of wholesome weeknight dinners at home; and khichadi paratha is a nod to my ba, who made magic out of leftovers and turned everyday meals into something unforgettable.

These recipes are approachable and adaptable, designed for home cooks with real-life time constraints. They're also immensely rewarding—whether you're serving them with one of the curries from chapter 1 or simply enjoying them warm from the pan, just like my family does.

As with the baked goods in the chapter to follow, I strongly recommend weighing your flour for best results here.

# GARLIC NAAN

Makes 8 to 9 naan

No Indian curry cookbook would be complete without a naan recipe—and for good reason. Soft, slightly chewy, and blistered in all the right places, naan is the perfect companion to rich, saucy dishes like tikka masala (page 37) or korma (page 63). This version is tailored for the home cook, using a skillet on the stovetop to mimic the high heat of a traditional tandoor (clay oven). The result is warm, pillowy flatbread with just enough char to make every bite irresistible. If you happen to have a home pizza oven, even better—follow the manufacturer's instructions for cooking at high heat and bring it even closer to restaurant-style perfection.

1 cup (240 ml) unsweetened soy milk
800 grams (6½ cups) all-purpose flour, plus more as needed
7 grams (2½ teaspoons) instant yeast
2 teaspoons cane sugar
1 tablespoon plus 1 teaspoon neutral oil, divided
Salt
2 tablespoons finely chopped fresh cilantro leaves and stems
3 garlic cloves, minced (about 1 tablespoon)
2 to 3 tablespoons vegan butter, for serving

1. Heat the soy milk and 1 cup (240 ml) water in a medium saucepan over medium heat or in a small bowl in the microwave until lukewarm. Set aside to cool slightly if too hot.
2. Place the flour in a large bowl. Add the yeast, sugar, 1 tablespoon oil, and 1 teaspoon salt, and mix with your fingers until well combined. Add the soy-milk-and-water mixture and knead with your hands into a soft dough. Add more water or flour, 1 teaspoon at a time, if the dough becomes too dry or wet to work with. Continue kneading until the dough springs back slightly when you apply pressure with your finger, 5 to 10 minutes. Alternatively, use a stand mixer with the dough hook attachment and mix on medium-low for about 5 minutes.
3. Coat the dough in the remaining 1 teaspoon oil and then cover with a silicone lid or plastic wrap. Keep at warm room temperature (or in the oven with the light on) until doubled in size, 1 to 2 hours.
4. Divide the dough into eight or nine pieces (about 150 grams each), and form into balls. Transfer to a tray and cover with a clean, moist kitchen towel.
5. Working with one dough ball at a time, dust the ball with flour and use a rolling pin to roll it out into a circle or oval shape on a board or counter. Lift the dough after every few rolls, and dust more as needed to prevent sticking. Roll the dough out to ¼ to ½ inch (6 mm to 1 cm) thick.
6. Heat a large nonstick pan over medium heat. Sprinkle an even layer of cilantro and garlic over the rolled dough (top side only) and press it into the surface with your fingers. Place the rolled dough on the hot pan garlic-and-cilantro side up, lower the heat slightly, and cook until bubbles form on the top and the bottom is browned, about 2 minutes. Watch closely and lower the heat if needed to prevent burning. Flip and cook until browned on the other side, 1 to 2 minutes. Remove from the heat.
7. Spread about 1 teaspoon vegan butter on top. Set aside and cover with a clean kitchen towel (or wrap in foil) to keep warm. Repeat steps 6 and 7 for the remaining dough balls.

8 Cut each piece of naan into quarters and serve immediately. Store leftover naan in a resealable plastic bag or airtight container in the refrigerator for up to 3 days or in the freezer for up to 3 months. To reheat, place a large nonstick pan over low-medium heat. Add the naan and cook on both sides until heated through, 1 to 2 minutes per side if refrigerated or 3 to 4 minutes per side if frozen.

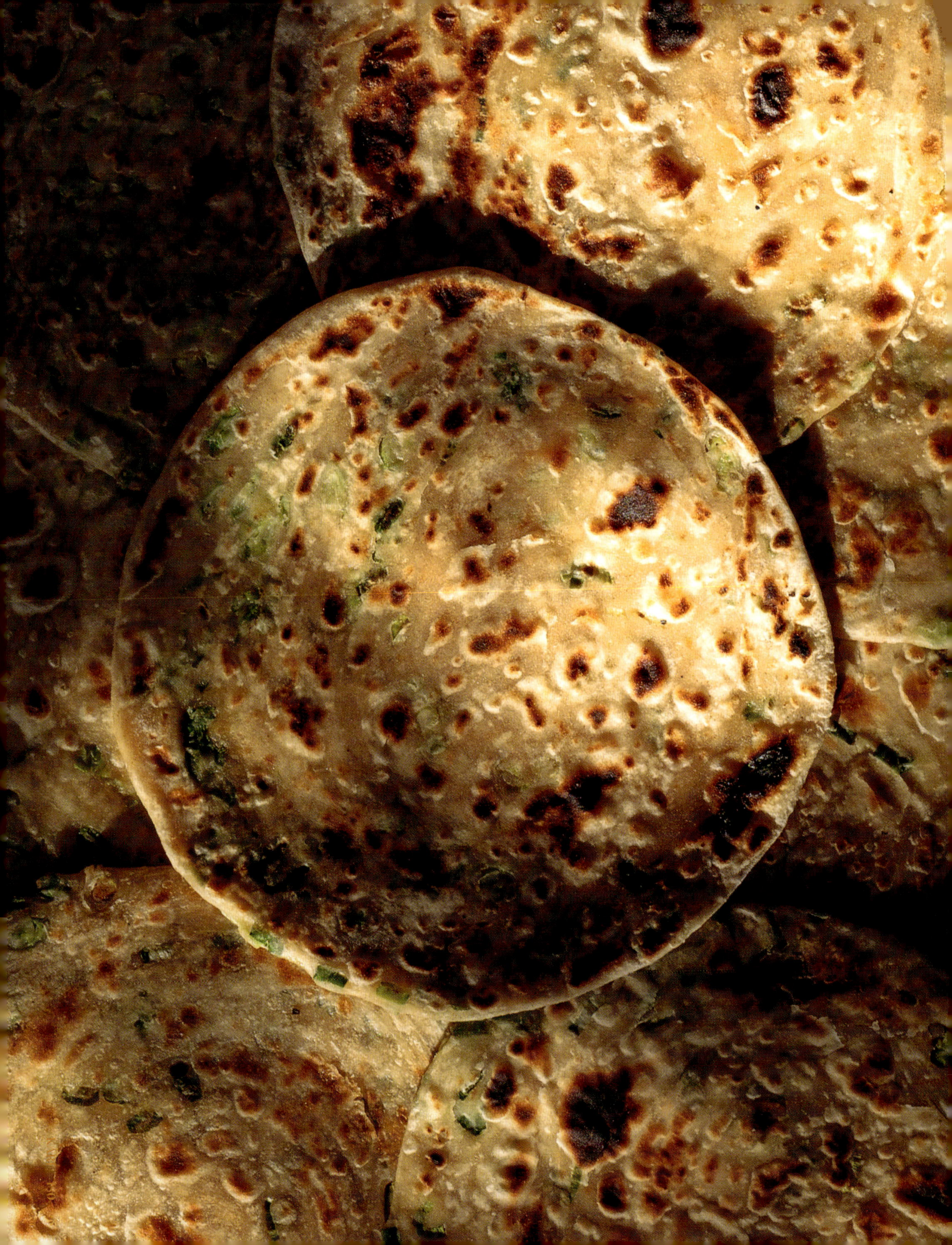

# FLAKY SCALLION PARATHA

Makes 12 paratha

This layered flatbread is inspired by the technique behind Chinese scallion pancakes and two beloved Indian flatbreads: lachha paratha from the North, made with atta (Indian whole wheat flour), and Malabar parotta from the South, typically made with all-purpose flour. I've blended elements from all three to create a flaky, flavorful flatbread that's both familiar and incredibly versatile. Because the flavor of scallions goes well with all things Asian, this is a go-to bread for soaking up pretty much any curry from chapter 1, but you can also serve it with my Fall Daal (page 161) or French Lentils with Lemon Rosemary Tadka (page 162) for a heartier meal.

350 grams (2¾ cups) all-purpose flour, plus 2 tablespoons for sprinkling and more for dusting
200 grams (1½ cups) atta or whole wheat flour
Salt
135 ml (½ cup plus 1 tablespoon) neutral oil, divided
8 scallions, thinly sliced

1. Mix the all-purpose flour, atta, ½ teaspoon salt, and 1 tablespoon oil in a large bowl with a wooden spoon or clean fingers. Add 360 milliliters (1½ cups) warm water slowly, continuing to mix to form a soft dough, about 1 minute. Add more water or all-purpose flour, 1 teaspoon at a time, if the dough becomes too dry or wet to work with. Knead until well combined, about 5 minutes.
2. Coat the dough in about 1 teaspoon oil and then cover with a silicone lid or plastic wrap. Allow the dough to rest for about 30 minutes.
3. Divide the dough into twelve pieces (about 75 grams each), and form into balls. Transfer to a plate and cover with a clean, moist kitchen towel.
4. Work with one dough ball at a time and keep the remaining dough covered. Dust the dough ball with a light sprinkle of all-purpose flour and roll into an 8-inch (20 cm) circle on a board or counter. Brush about 1 teaspoon oil on top in a thin layer and then sprinkle evenly with ½ teaspoon all-purpose flour and 2 tablespoons scallions. Working from one side to the other, roll the dough into a thick log and then coil it tightly to form a round. Flatten the round with your palm, sprinkle with a light dusting of all-purpose flour on both sides, and roll into a thin 7-inch (18 cm) circle.
5. Heat a large nonstick pan over medium heat. Reduce the heat to medium-low, place the rolled paratha on the hot pan, and cook until brown spots form on the bottom, about 1 minute. Flip and brush about ½ teaspoon oil on top. Continue to cook until browned on the other side, about 30 seconds. Flip and brush ½ teaspoon oil on the other side. Flip again and continue to cook for a few more seconds to allow the oil to absorb.
6. For softer paratha (better for scooping up curry), transfer to a plate and cover with a clean kitchen towel (or wrap in foil) to keep warm. For flakier paratha (with thinner layers, perfect for dipping into thinner curries), place the paratha onto a clean kitchen towel after cooking, scrunch a few times, and transfer to a wire rack to cool.
7. Repeat steps 4 to 6 to roll out and cook the remaining dough balls (see Tip). Serve immediately.

**TIP**

As you get a hang of the technique, you can save time by rolling out the next paratha while the previous one is cooking. This is also easier if you have a friend to help.

# KHICHADI PARATHA

Makes 6 paratha

Have leftover Sushi Rice Khichadi (page 165)? This comforting recipe is a smart and tasty way to give it new life. According to my dad, my ba (his mother) not only dreamed up the idea of turning leftover khichadi into this flatbread but also won a cooking competition in India with it. I can't say for sure whether she was the original inventor, but it's a story I love—and the result speaks for itself. The khichadi is made into a dough with atta, a finely ground Indian whole wheat flour, and then made into wholesome and hearty flatbreads. If you don't have atta, you can use an equal mix of whole wheat and all-purpose flour instead.

1 cup (250 g) Sushi Rice Khichadi (page 165), refrigerated overnight
1¼ cup (150 g) atta, plus more for dusting and kneading
1 tablespoon white sesame seeds, optional
½ teaspoon garam masala
½ teaspoon gochugaru or ¼ teaspoon ground red chili, to taste
Salt
3 tablespoons neutral oil, divided
Mango Miso Masala Chutney (page 86), nondairy yogurt, or achar (Indian pickles), for serving

1. Place the Sushi Rice Khichadi, atta, sesame seeds (if using), garam masala, and gochugaru and ½ teaspoon salt in a large bowl. Stir with a spoon until the atta is incorporated and then knead until well combined into a soft dough, about 5 minutes. If the dough becomes too sticky, knead in more atta, 1 tablespoon at a time.
2. Coat the dough in about 1 teaspoon oil and then cover with a silicone lid or plastic wrap. Allow the dough to rest for about 15 minutes.
3. Divide the dough into six pieces (about 65 grams each), and form balls. Transfer to a plate and cover with a clean, moist kitchen towel.
4. Work with one dough ball at a time and leave the rest covered. Dust the dough ball with atta and use a rolling pin to roll it out into a 6-inch (15 cm) circle on a board or counter. Lift the dough after every few rolls, and dust more as needed to prevent sticking.
5. Heat a large nonstick pan over medium heat. Place the dough on the hot pan, reduce the heat to medium-low, and cook until brown spots form on the bottom, about 1 minute. Flip and brush on about ½ teaspoon oil. Continue to cook until browned on the other side, 15 to 30 seconds. Flip and brush on ½ teaspoon oil. Flip again and continue to cook for a few more seconds to allow the oil to absorb. Transfer to a plate and cover with a clean kitchen towel (or wrap in foil) to keep warm.
6. Repeat steps 4 and 5 to roll out and cook the remaining dough balls (see Tip). Serve immediately with Mango Miso Masala Chutney or as desired.

**TIP**
As you get a hang of the technique, you can save time by rolling out the next paratha while the previous one is cooking. This is also easier if you have a friend to help.

# DRINKS & DESSERTS

I'm not ashamed to admit I have a sweet tooth. I can't consider a day complete without at least a little something sweet—even if it's just a handful of in-season berries or a square of velvety dark chocolate. It's not about over-indulgence but rather about celebration, comfort, and joy.

In this chapter, I present much more than just berries. I invite you into my dessert world, where familiar cravings meet unexpected twists. These are my all-star, time-tested, family-approved treats—desserts that I return to again and again to share with family and friends, not only because they're delicious but because they bring people together.

I consider these American-ish sweets with Indo-Asian flair. You'll find familiar favorites—beverage syrups, baked goods, and a frozen treat—but they're infused with flavors and fruits often found in Indian and Asian desserts such as cardamom, saffron, lychee, and mango. These flavors echo the Indian and Asian desserts I grew up with or discovered through travels and family stories—but they've been re-imagined for the modern, curious palate. I encourage you to take these recipes and run with them: Experiment with different flavors and have fun!

To make all the baked recipes in this chapter, you'll need a kitchen scale (sorry, not sorry about this—if you want to have success with home baking and these recipes, you will need one). I've begrudgingly added imperial measurements (i.e., cups of flour), but the exact weight of a cup of flour can vary vastly among home cooks. You'll also need two 8-inch (20 cm) round pans (I like USA Pan brand)—with optional 8-inch (20 cm) round parchment sheets—and a 9 × 5-inch (23 × 13 cm) loaf pan.

# BROWN SUGAR MASALA SYRUP

Makes 1 cup (240 ml)

Ever since I became a parent to three young children, I have run on morning lattes (espresso with oat or soy milk, with a splash of flavored syrup) both for the caffeine and the 1-minute meditative ritual that making it provides. I like making my own flavored syrup at home every couple of weeks (there's always a bottle or two in my fridge), since I like to switch up the flavors for my morning latte. I developed this recipe for brown sugar masala syrup, which has a lot of the spices used in chai, to add a similar depth of flavor and comfort that chai has. Sometimes I prefer just cinnamon or cardamom instead of the combination of spices, so feel free to play around with the spice ratio here. It can also be used as a sweetener for tea or as a replacement for chai masala and sugar in a traditional masala chai recipe (you can find a recipe for masala chai in my first cookbook, *Plant-Based India*).

- 1 small cinnamon stick
- 1 tablespoon green cardamom pods
- 1 small piece mace or ¼ teaspoon ground nutmeg, optional
- 5 cloves
- 1 teaspoon fennel seeds
- ½ teaspoon black peppercorns
- 1 cup (220 g) packed light brown sugar
- 1 tablespoon minced ginger
- Pinch of salt

1. Coarsely grind the cinnamon, cardamom, mace (if using), cloves, fennel seeds, and peppercorns with a mortar and pestle (or spice grinder).
2. Heat a medium saucepan over medium heat. Add the spices and toast, stirring frequently, until fragrant, 30 to 60 seconds. Add 2 cups (480 ml) water, the brown sugar, ginger, and salt.
3. Stir well to combine and bring to a boil. Stir until the sugar is fully dissolved, about 5 minutes.
4. Reduce the heat to low to maintain a gentle simmer. Simmer until the flavors from the spices have infused and the mixture thickens to a syrupy consistency, about 30 minutes.
5. Use a fine-mesh strainer to strain the syrup into an airtight glass container and allow to cool to room temperature. Use as desired or store in the refrigerator for up to 1 week.

# CURRY LEAF SYRUP

Makes 1¼ cups (300 ml)

In case you don't have enough uses for curry leaves by now, here's one more to round it all out. Curry leaves (see page 20) are used extensively across India. They have such a wonderful earthy yet floral flavor that is essential in many Indian dishes. You'll largely find them in savory applications, but I've found they make an incredible flavored syrup! Add a splash of this syrup to your favorite citrus sparkling water and pair with any of the curries in this book. It's a great sweetener for a matcha latte, since the citrusy, earthy flavor of the curry leaf highlights the herbal, grassy notes of matcha. You could also use pandan leaves or makrut lime leaves in place of curry leaves to make a syrup for a floral, sparkling water drink that would complement Southeast Asian–inspired dishes like my Lemongrass Yellow Curry (page 51).

25 fresh curry leaves, torn or thinly sliced
1 cup (200 g) cane sugar
Salt

1. Heat the curry leaves, sugar, ¼ teaspoon salt, and 1½ cups (360 ml) water in a medium saucepan over high heat. Stir well to combine and bring to a boil. Reduce the heat to medium-low and simmer, stirring occasionally, until fragrant and thickened to a loose, syrupy consistency, about 10 minutes.
2. Remove from the heat and let stand to cool, about 15 minutes.
3. Use a fine-mesh strainer to strain the syrup into an airtight glass container and allow to cool to room temperature. Use as desired or store in the refrigerator for up to 1 week.

# RASPBERRY ROSE SYRUP

Makes ¾ cup (180 ml)

Rooh Afza is one of the most popular brands of rose syrup used in drinks and desserts across South Asia. Here's my slightly less sweet version of the classic that relies on rose water for flavor and raspberry for color and a friendly tang. Mix 1 to 2 tablespoons of syrup (or to taste) with cold still or sparkling water, or nondairy milk of your choice, for a refreshing beverage on a hot day. It can also be drizzled over vanilla ice cream.

1 cup (140 g) frozen raspberries
½ cup (100 g) cane sugar
1 tablespoon dried rose petals
1 tablespoon rose water

1. Heat the raspberries, sugar, and rose petals and 1 cup (240 ml) water in a medium saucepan over medium-high heat. Stir well and bring to a boil. Reduce the heat to medium-low and simmer, stirring occasionally, until the sugar completely dissolves and the mixture thickens to a loose, syrupy consistency, about 8 minutes. Stir in the rose water and remove from the heat.
2. Use a fine-mesh strainer to strain the syrup into an airtight glass container, pressing thoroughly to pass through the raspberry pulp (see Note), and allow to cool to room temperature. Use as desired or store in the refrigerator for up to 1 week.

**NOTE**
Don't discard the raspberry seeds; they can be used as a topping for oatmeal, toast, or yogurt.

# LYCHEE COCONUT GRANITA

Serves 6 to 8

Granita, an icy Italian dessert made by scraping a frozen liquid made from water, sugar, fruit, or other flavorings, is easy to make at home since all you need is a pan and a fork. Lychee is one of my all-time favorite fruits—sweet, juicy, floral, and bright—so it's the star of this granita, which is akin to Asian frozen desserts like ice gola (Indian shaved ice) and Korean bingsu (shaved milk-based ice with various toppings). If you've never had lychee or any of these desserts, let this be your introduction. Since fresh lychees are not available year-round (at least in the Midwest), I've called upon the reliable canned lychees in syrup, which you can source from your local Asian supermarket or online. Coconut milk not only rounds out the flavor of this granita but also offers a mellow mouthfeel that makes it the perfect palate cleanser or light dessert. You can either enjoy it on its own or dress up with edible flowers for a special occasion. You can also use this granita as a topping for fresh fruit such as berries, diced mangoes, or diced melon. You'll need a few hours for the granita to freeze, but it is worth the wait.

One 20-ounce (567 g) can lychees in syrup
One 13.5-ounce (400 ml) can coconut milk
Salt
Edible flowers, optional, for garnish

1. Combine the lychees with syrup, coconut milk, and ¼ teaspoon salt in a blender. Blend until smooth.
2. Transfer to an 8-inch (20 cm) square ceramic or glass tray with a lid. Cover and place in the freezer for 1 to 2 hours, until the mixture starts to freeze on the sides and top.
3. Remove from the freezer and use a fork to scrape up the ice crystals. Return to the freezer for 1 to 2 hours more, until mostly frozen, and scrape up the ice crystals again. Store in the freezer for up to 1 week.
4. When ready to serve, scrape the granita and scoop into serving cups. Top with edible flowers, if using, and serve immediately.

# ROSE CHOCOLATE COOKIE CAKE

Makes two 8-inch (20 cm) cookie cakes

This is my tried-and-true cookie cake recipe. I make it all the time for birthdays, holidays, and dinner parties. I like baking the cakes in two 8-inch (20 cm) rounds for a few reasons. You can easily keep half the dough in the fridge and bake the second cake a couple days later (the dough keeps in the fridge for up to 5 days). It's also a bit more forgiving if you underbake it, because then it can just be enjoyed family-style with spoons straight from the pan. Also, if you're going to take the time to make cookie dough, you might as well make enough for two cakes.

Since rose is a flavor used extensively in desserts across South Asia, I was inspired to add rose water and petals here to dress up the chocolate chip base recipe. The subtle floral notes help bring out the fruitiness of the dark chocolate. However, you could easily omit the rose and stick with just dark chocolate (or any other chocolate you like). Feel free to make it your own by using other add-ins such as chopped nuts, dried fruits, sprinkles, candied ginger, and spices (see Note)!

The cookie cake is great on its own, but you can also decorate it with my vegan buttercream (page 199).

410 grams (3¼ cups) all-purpose flour
1 tablespoon cornstarch
1 teaspoon baking soda
½ teaspoon baking powder
226 grams (1 cup) vegan butter, softened
220 grams (1 cup packed) light brown sugar
200 grams (1 cup) cane sugar
80 milliliters (⅓ cup) unsweetened plain soy or oat milk
2 teaspoons vanilla bean paste or extract
1 teaspoon rose water
¼ teaspoon ground cardamom
Salt
100 grams (about ¾ cup) dark chocolate chips or chunks, plus more for topping
2 tablespoons dried rose petals

1. Preheat the oven to 350°F (180°C). Line two 8-inch (20 cm) round baking pans with parchment paper.
2. Whisk together the flour, cornstarch, baking soda, and baking powder in a large bowl.
3. Cream together the butter, brown sugar, and cane sugar with an electric hand mixer or in a stand mixer on medium speed until light and fluffy, 3 to 5 minutes. (If you don't have an electric mixer, you can use a whisk.) Add the soy milk, vanilla, rose water, and cardamom and ¼ teaspoon salt, and mix well on low speed to combine.
4. Incorporate the flour mixture on low speed to form an evenly mixed dough. Mix in the chocolate chips and rose petals on low speed to distribute evenly throughout.
5. Divide the dough evenly between the two baking pans. Press the dough with your fingers to form an even layer. Press a few additional chocolate chips into the top of the dough.
6. Bake for 35 to 40 minutes, until the top is golden brown and an inserted toothpick comes out mostly clean.
7. Remove from the oven, let cool for about 5 minutes, and then invert onto a wire rack to finish cooling. Serve warm or at room temperature. Store in an airtight container at room temperature for up to 3 days.

**NOTE**

Here are some different mix-in combinations to inspire you on your cookie cake journey. You can add as much of any of these ingredients as you like, as long as they are evenly distributed through the dough.

- Chopped pistachios, orange blossom water (in place of rose water), and semisweet chocolate chips
- Chopped walnuts or hazelnuts and any chocolate
- Dark chocolate, orange zest, and candied ginger
- Semisweet chocolate chips and candied fennel
- Chopped dried mango and nondairy white chocolate chips
- Dark chocolate and chai masala

**NOTES**

1 Here are some additional ideas for variations on this cake. For all of these options, omit the lemon zest, saffron, and rose water. You can also use apple cider vinegar in place of lemon juice.

- Make a simple vanilla cake (no add-ins; be sure to use the best-quality vanilla you can find)
- Add sprinkles into the batter
- Add 2 tablespoons cocoa powder or matcha powder in with the flour
- Mix black and/or white sesame seeds into the batter
- Keep the lemon zest or replace with orange zest and add poppy seeds

2 If you need enough buttercream to coat the sides of the cake and to decorate the top with a piping bag, simply double the recipe.

# LEMON SAFFRON CAKE

Makes two 8-inch (20 cm) cake layers

This is my all-time favorite homemade cake recipe. I use olive oil and almond flour to give it a tender and moist crumb. After tasting this cake (and several flavor variations of it), my family has unanimously agreed that I will be the designated cake-baker for all birthdays in the family. The lemon offers a wonderful brightness that complements the floral notes and rich color of saffron. I've used two 8-inch (20 cm) round pans here, which allows me to make a simple layer cake with ease. I top this cake with a not-too-sweet vegan buttercream and fresh fruit. As with the cookie cake recipe on page 196, use this recipe as a starting point and feel free to play around with the flavors (see Note 1).

275 grams (1¼ cups) cane sugar
2 teaspoons lemon zest (from about 2 lemons)
½ teaspoon saffron
280 grams (2¼ cups) all-purpose flour
50 grams (½ cup) almond flour
1 teaspoon baking powder
½ teaspoon baking soda
Salt
360 ml (1½ cups) unsweetened plain soy milk
120 ml (½ cup) olive oil
2 tablespoons lemon juice (from about 1 lemon)
2 teaspoons vanilla bean paste or extract
1 tablespoon rose water

### VEGAN BUTTERCREAM (SEE NOTE 2)

150 grams (1¼ cups) sifted powdered sugar
113 grams (½ cup) salted vegan butter, softened
½ teaspoon rose water
½ teaspoon vanilla extract

### FOR SERVING

Fresh fruit (such as diced mango or whole berries)
Edible flowers, optional
Edible gold leaf, optional

1. Preheat the oven to 350°F (180°C). Line two 8-inch (20 cm) round baking pans with parchment paper.
2. Place the cane sugar and lemon zest in a large bowl and rub them between your fingers to combine until evenly distributed and very lemony in fragrance, about 1 minute. Crush the saffron between your fingers and add it to the sugar mixture. Then, sift in the all-purpose flour, almond flour, baking powder, baking soda, and ¼ teaspoon salt, and whisk to combine.
3. Whisk together the soy milk, oil, lemon juice, vanilla, and rose water in a medium bowl.
4. Slowly add the liquid to the dry mixture and combine with a spatula to form a batter. It's okay if some small lumps remain; it is more important not to overmix the batter.
5. Distribute the batter between the two lined baking pans. Use a spatula to spread it out evenly.
6. Bake for 20 minutes, rotate the pans, and bake for 10 to 15 minutes more, until an inserted toothpick comes out clean or with dry crumbs.
7. Allow the cakes to cool for about 5 minutes and then invert onto a wire rack. Let cool completely, about 1 hour.
8. Once the cakes are nearly cooled, prepare the buttercream: Whisk together the powdered sugar, vegan butter, rose water, and vanilla extract until light and fluffy, about 5 minutes.
9. To assemble the cake, spread about half of the buttercream on top of one cake and top with the second cake. Top with the remaining buttercream and the fruit, and decorate with edible flowers and gold leaf, if using.
10. The cake will keep in an airtight container in the refrigerator for 3 to 5 days. Remove from the refrigerator 1 to 2 hours before serving; the taste and texture are best at room temperature.

# CHAI MASALA CARROT LOAF

## *with Rose Water Glaze*

Makes one loaf cake

Since carrot cake is usually flavored with spices like cinnamon and nutmeg, I've leaned into this further by adding a chai masala, a warm blend of ground spices (such as cinnamon, cardamom, ginger, and black pepper) used to make chai. This spice blend, which you can find readily at Indian grocery stores or online, turns this carrot loaf into the perfect dessert to enjoy on a crisp fall day. The sweeter spices like cinnamon and cardamom bring out the natural sweetness of the carrots, and the ginger and black pepper offer a subtle and welcome heat. While it's not quite the same, you can sub in pumpkin spice or apple pie spice for the chai masala for an equally delicious spiced carrot loaf. Just don't skip the rose water glaze—it adds a lovely floral brightness to the rich, earthy cake.

325 grams (2⅔ cups) all-purpose flour
220 grams (1 cup packed) light brown sugar
1 tablespoon chai masala
1 tablespoon cornstarch
1 teaspoon baking powder
½ teaspoon baking soda
Salt
240 ml (1 cup) unsweetened plain soy milk
120 ml (½ cup) olive oil
1½ tablespoons lemon juice (from about 1 small lemon)
1½ teaspoons vanilla bean paste or extract
150 grams (1½ cups) grated carrot (about 3 or 4 medium carrots)

### ROSE WATER GLAZE

120 grams (1 cup) powdered sugar
2 teaspoons rose water

### FOR SERVING, OPTIONAL

Edible gold leaf
Dried rose petals
Chai masala

1. Preheat the oven to 350°F (180°C). Line a 9 × 5-inch (23 × 13 cm) loaf pan with parchment paper.
2. Whisk together the flour, brown sugar, chai masala, cornstarch, baking powder, and baking soda and ¼ teaspoon salt in a large bowl.
3. Whisk together the soy milk, oil, lemon juice, and vanilla in a medium bowl.
4. Slowly add the liquid to the dry mixture and combine with a spatula to form a thick batter. Gently stir in the carrots and then transfer to the loaf pan.
5. Bake for 65 to 70 minutes, rotating the pan halfway through, until an inserted toothpick comes out clean or with dry crumbs.
6. Allow the cake to cool for about 5 minutes and then invert onto a wire rack. Let cool completely, about 2 hours.
7. The cake will keep in an airtight container in the refrigerator for 3 to 5 days. Remove from the refrigerator 1 to 2 hours before serving; the taste and texture are best at room temperature.
8. When ready to serve, make the rose water glaze: Whisk together the powdered sugar and rose water, adding water ½ teaspoon at a time, to form a thick glaze. Cut the cake into 1-inch (2.5 cm) slices (or to desired thickness). Transfer the slices to serving plates and drizzle each slice with the glaze to taste. Top with gold leaf, rose petals, and a sprinkling of chai masala, if using, and serve.

# MENUS

## SPRING REFRESH

A vibrant collection that welcomes the season of renewal. Think bright flavors, crisp textures, and feel-good dishes to shake off winter's heaviness.

- Tofu Katsu Makhani (page 33)
- Spring Khichadi (page 166)
- Sparkling water with Curry Leaf Syrup (page 191)

## LATE SUMMER

A celebration of summer brightness featuring a wholesome main, a light side, and a refreshing dessert.

- French Lentils with Lemon Rosemary Tadka (page 162)
- Zucchini Corn Pakoras with Mango Miso Masala Chutney (page 89)
- Lychee Coconut Granita (page 195)

## HEARTY FALL

As the air cools and cravings deepen, this feast leans into cozy spices and comforting textures to celebrate autumn's harvest.

- Braised Miso Tofu and Onions with Cauliflower Puree (page 78)
- Fall Daal (page 161)
- Brussels Sprout Pakoras with Cranberry Chutney (page 94)
- Endive Apple Salad with Chili Lime Tadka Dressing (page 108)

## COZY WINTER

Warming, grounding, and deeply nourishing—this menu is designed for cold days when you crave something hearty but still bright.

- Sushi Rice Khichadi (page 165)
- Roasted Squash with Chili Lime Tadka Dressing (page 111)
- Chai Masala Carrot Loaf with Rose Water Glaze (page 200)

## GREEN MACHINE

A celebration of all things green and vibrant. These dishes pack in herbs, leafy veggies, and sauces that make eating your greens deliciously easy.

- Chana Saag (page 59)
- Spring Khichadi (page 166)
- Roasted Vegetables with Green Chutney Tahini Sauce (page 101)

## AN ODE TO ROOT VEG

Root vegetables are earthy, sweet, and versatile. This menu honors their grounding presence with dishes that let them shine in unexpected ways.

- Crispy Potatoes with Peanut Coconut Curry (page 45)
- Beet Korma with Tofu and Cauliflower (page 64)
- Carrot, Pistachio, and Mint Salad (page 120)
- Flaky Scallion Paratha (page 181)

## INDIAN RESTAURANT CLASSICS

Inspired by restaurant favorites: familiar, nostalgic, and full of flavor.

- Tofu Tikka Masala (page 38)
- Fluffy Basmati Rice (page 154)
- Garlic Naan (page 178)

## GAME DAY (GAME OPTIONAL) OR FUN BIRTHDAY

These playful, crowd-pleasing recipes are perfect for celebrations big and small—whether you're watching a game or just hanging out with friends.

- Makhani Nachos (page 34)
- Green Pea Tikkis with Cranberry Chutney (page 97)
- Rose Chocolate Cookie Cake (page 196)

## WEEKEND PASTA DINNER

With rich sauces, familiar carbs, and a few unexpected twists, this meal is for slow weekend evenings and comfort-filled plates.

- Lemony Tofu "Ricotta" Stuffed Shells (page 135)
- Beans, Greens, and Grains Salad (page 123)
- Crusty bread

## A TRIP TO SOUTHEAST ASIA

Aromatic, punchy, and packed with contrast, these recipes draw inspiration from the vibrant flavors and cooking techniques of Southeast Asian kitchens.

- Lemongrass Yellow Curry with Silken Tofu and Peas (page 52)
- Curry Fried Rice (page 170)
- Lychee Coconut Granita (page 195)

## GRILL GATHERING

Smoky, charred, tangy, and bold—this lineup is made for the grill, the picnic table, or anywhere you gather under the sun with a plate in hand.

- Roasted Red Pepper and Giardiniera Panini with Saag (page 60)
- Grilled Squash and Eggplant with Lemony Tofu "Ricotta" and Chili Crisp Panko (page 132)
- Grilled Corn with Lemon Pepper Glaze (page 149)

# MIDWEST FARMERS MARKET VEGETABLE INDEX

Where I live, in the north suburbs of Chicago, I'm lucky to have access to many great farmers markets from May through October. Eating locally benefits small businesses, reduces your carbon footprint, and tastes better, too! If possible, I encourage you to seek out farmers markets near you.

This guide lists produce that is local to me, but anyone can use it to come up with ideas about how to use farmers market produce! If you don't have access to a farmers market, you can still use this as a general guide for cooking with supermarket produce.

## ASPARAGUS

- Spring Khichadi (page 166)

## BEETS

- Beet Korma with Tofu and Cauliflower (page 64)
- Beet Korma Pasta with Lemony Garlic Breadcrumbs (page 67)
- Fall Daal (page 161; replace the squash with beets)

## BELL PEPPERS

- Tikka Masala Bread Pizza (page 41)
- Uttapam with Peanut Coconut Curry (page 46)
- Roasted Vegetables with Green Chutney Tahini Sauce (page 101)
- Fiery Bean and Vegetable Soup (page 158)
- Curry Fried Rice (page 170)
- Curry Noodle Stir Fry (page 173)

## BROCCOLI

- Lemongrass Yellow Curry Noodle Soup with Tempeh (page 55)
- Roasted Vegetables with Green Chutney Tahini Sauce (page 101)
- Creamy Five Spice Rice Bowl (page 128)
- Lemon Pepper Tofu and Broccoli (page 146)
- Curry Fried Rice (page 170)

## BRUSSELS SPROUTS

- Brussels Sprout Pakoras with Cranberry Chutney (page 94)

## CABBAGE

- Tofu Katsu Makhani (page 33)
- Crispy Chickpea Salad with Green Chutney Tahini Sauce (page 102)
- Tofu Lettuce Wrap Salad with Carrot Ginger Dressing (page 116)
- Vegetable Pancakes with Manchurian Sauce (page 139)
- Vegetable Wontons with Manchurian Sauce (page 140)
- Curry Noodle Stir Fry (page 173)

## CARROTS

- Roasted Vegetables with Green Chutney Tahini Sauce (page 101)
- Edamame and Crisp Lettuce Salad with Carrot Ginger Dressing (page 115)
- Tofu Lettuce Wrap Salad with Carrot Ginger Dressing (page 116)

- Carrot, Pistachio, and Mint Salad (page 120)
- Creamy Five Spice Noodles (page 127)
- Vegetable Pancakes with Manchurian Sauce (page 139)
- Vegetable Wontons with Manchurian Sauce (page 140)
- Fiery Bean and Vegetable Soup (page 158)
- Curry Noodle Stir Fry (page 173)
- Chai Masala Carrot Loaf with Rose Water Glaze (page 200)

## CAULIFLOWER

- Beet Korma with Tofu and Cauliflower (page 64)
- Madras Cauliflower (page 73)
- Braised Miso Tofu and Onions with Cauliflower Puree (page 78)
- Fettuccine in Tadka Cauliflower Sauce (page 81)
- Mango Miso Masala Glazed Cauliflower with Quinoa (page 90)
- Roasted Vegetables with Green Chutney Tahini Sauce (page 101)

## CORN

- Zucchini Corn Pakoras with Mango Miso Masala Chutney (page 89)
- Grilled Corn with Lemon Pepper Glaze (page 149)

## EGGPLANT

- Grilled Squash and Eggplant with Lemony Tofu "Ricotta" and Chili Crisp Panko (page 132)

## GREENS

- Spinach and Herb Saag (page 56)
- Crispy Chickpea Salad with Green Chutney Tahini Sauce (page 102)
- Beans, Greens, and Grains Salad (page 123)

## MUSHROOMS

- Seared Maitake Mushrooms with Madras Curry (page 74)
- Mushroom Rice (page 157)

## ONIONS

- Tikka Masala Bread Pizza (page 41)
- Uttapam with Peanut Coconut Curry (page 46)
- Braised Miso Tofu and Onions with Cauliflower Puree (page 78)
- Vegetable Pancakes with Manchurian Sauce (page 139)
- . . . and pretty much any recipe in this book

## PEAS

- Lemongrass Yellow Curry with Silken Tofu and Peas (page 52)
- Green Pea Tikkis with Cranberry Chutney (page 97)

## POTATOES

- Crispy Potatoes with Peanut Coconut Curry (page 45)
- Green Pea Tikkis with Cranberry Chutney (page 97)
- Fiery Bean and Vegetable Soup (page 158)

# REFLECTIONS ON ART: PLATING, POTTERY, AND TEXTILES

Cooking can be a meditative process and a form of artistic expression. I hope that this cookbook inspires you to express your own creativity through preparing these recipes.

You don't really need fancy equipment to plate food in a thoughtful way. I often say my favorite kitchen utensil is my hands! Tweezers are completely optional in most cases but can be nice to have for more delicate garnishes.

Some things I like to use for garnishing:

- Microgreens, sliced scallions, or torn herbs such as mint or cilantro.
- Edible fresh flowers—whatever I can source locally or grow in my backyard. Some examples of edible flowers are rose, marigold, and jasmine. I like to look for flowers that have specifically been grown to be eaten as opposed to what you might find in a store's floral department. For special occasions or events, I source online through Gourmet Sweet Botanicals.
- Dry flowers such as dried rose petals.
- Paprika or chili flakes such as gochugaru (see page 17).
- Chili threads (also known as silgochu; very thinly sliced red Korean chili).
- Seeds such as sesame seeds or hemp seeds.
- Tadka (see page 20).

Pottery is also an important aspect of presenting dishes. Handmade pottery brings so much life and soul to a home. I'm proud to say nearly every piece of ceramicware photographed in this book is handmade by one of the following local Chicagoland potters/ceramic artists:

- Monsoon Pottery by Danielle Chutinthranond (@monsoonpottery)
- This Quiet Dust Ceramics by Dubhe Carreño (@thisquietdustceramicsbydubhe)
- DTK Ceramics by David T. Kim (@dtkceramics)

I've also included a handful of pieces from Golden Ratio Clay Works by Soula Pefkaros (@goldenratioclayworks), who created the iconic ceramic thali set featured on the cover of my first cookbook, *Plant-Based India.*

All four of these artists sell their work online, and I'd love for you to support their work and tell them I sent you!

The block-printed textiles in the photographs are sourced from Soil to Studio (@soiltostudio) and Filling Spaces (@fillingspacesdesigns).

# SUGGESTIONS FOR FURTHER READING AND EATING

My experiences as a cook and recipe developer have been shaped by many different things. Reading and cooking through the cookbooks and dining at the restaurants below have been instrumental in the development of this book.

## COOKBOOKS

These cookbooks have a permanent spot on my bookshelf.

*Amrikan* by Khushbu Shah

*Bangkok* by Leela Punyaratabandhu

*Big Vegan Flavor* by Nisha Vora

*Desi Bakes* by Hetal Vasavada

*Dishoom* by Shamil Thakrar, Kavi Thakrar, and Naved Nasir

*East* by Meera Sodha

*Ever-Green Vietnamese* by Andrea Nguyen

*First Generation* by Frankie Gaw

*I Am From Here* by Vishwesh Bhatt

*Indian-ish* by Priya Krishna

*Indian Flavor Every Day* by Maya Kaimal

*The Korean Vegan Cookbook* by Joanne Lee Molinaro

*Monsoon* by Asma Khan

*Mumbai Modern* by Amisha Dodhia Gurbani

*The Nutmeg Trail* by Eleanor Ford

*On the Curry Trail* by Raghavan Iyer

*PlantAsia* by Pamelia Chia

*Rambutan* by Cynthia Shanmugalingam

*Sabai* by Pailin Chongchitnant

*The Vegan Chinese Kitchen* by Hannah Che

*The Vibrant Hong Kong Table* by Christine Wong

## RESTAURANTS IN ILLINOIS

These are some of my favorite local Asian American restaurants that helped shape my palate for Asian American cuisine.

Alice & Friends (Chicago, Glenview)

altThai (Arlington Heights)

Bar Goa (Chicago)

Charoen Krung by Sathorn (Chicago)

Duck Duck Goat (Chicago)

Flambé India (Libertyville)

Gumrai Thai (Arlington Heights)

Indienne (Chicago)

Indus (Highland Park)

Mirra (Chicago)

Naansense (Chicago)

Nadu (Chicago)

PLANTA Queen (Chicago)

Roka Akor (Chicago, Skokie, Oak Brook)

ROOP (Chicago)

Swadesi (Chicago)

Thattu (Chicago)

Urban Vegan (Chicago)

## RESTAURANTS ACROSS THE US

By absolutely no means is this meant to be a comprehensive list of all the incredible Asian American restaurants in the US, but below are some I've been able to visit over the past few years. They've all played a role in providing inspiration for this book.

Besharam (San Francisco)

Hangawi (NYC)

Jade Rabbit (Portland)

Jing Fong (NYC)

Kajitsu (NYC; now closed)

The King and I (Milwaukee)

Kolkata Chai Co (NYC)

Minty Z (Miami; now closed)

Mirisata (Portland)

Obon Shokudo (Portland)

PLANTA (Miami; now closed)

Shizen (San Francisco)

# INDEX

# D



# E



# F



# G

# H



# I



# J



# K



# L

# M



# N



# O



# P

## Q



## R



## S

# T

# U



# V



# W



# Y



# Z

# ACKNOWLEDGMENTS

Shrey, Radhi, and Reva, my children: Thank you for giving me the greatest gift of fatherhood and the motivation to be the best version of myself every day. I've already learned so much from you. I look forward to creating many more wonderful food memories with you in the years to come.

Rachel, my wife: Thank you for your love and kindness and for also being my most eager taste-tester and editor. Thank you for tolerating me during my intense creative workdays and for helping me stay calm and humble through all of my pursuits, including writing this book. I'm so grateful to be on this journey of life together with you.

Dr. Sanjeev and Sonal Shukla, my parents: Thank you for your unconditional love and support for all that I do. I'm so glad you've been able to try pretty much all the recipes in this book. It is my greatest honor and pleasure to cook for you.

Pradip and Daxa Tailor, my in-laws, and my extended family: Thank you for your unwavering support and behind-the-scenes efforts in making this book a reality.

Charlie Brotherstone, my literary agent: Thank you for your guidance in navigating the world of publishing and for always knowing how to motivate me to move forward.

Olivia Peluso, editor extraordinaire and friend: Thank you for being you and for helping me shape this book into the best version possible. Thank you for giving me the editorial experience of my dreams (again!), trusting in my process, encouraging my creative freedom, and believing in me every step of the way.

The amazing team at DK, especially Mike Sanders, Ann Barton, Becky Batchelor, Bill Thomas, Resham Anand, West Matuszak, Bianca Bosman, Morgan Jefferson, and Beverlee Day: Thank you for sharing your expertise with me and providing the best home for this book.

Bee Berrie, master recipe tester: I could not have imagined a more perfect recipe tester for this book. Thank you so much for your enthusiasm for the book and for all of your constructive feedback.

My neighbors and friends: Thank you for being the best taste-testers and for helping consume the large quantities of food that come with recipe development.

My Instagram community: Thank you for engaging with my work over the years and giving me the platform to share my creativity with the world. I'm forever grateful.

# ABOUT THE AUTHOR

Sheil Shukla, DO, is a board-certified internal medicine physician and food artist. He is the creator, recipe developer, and food photographer of @plantbasedartist on Instagram. His culinary interests are in South Asian and East Asian cuisines, including the regional "thali" tradition of Gujarat, India; this is explored in more depth in his debut cookbook, *Plant-Based India: Nourishing Recipes Rooted in Tradition,* which was named a *New York Times* Best Cookbook of 2022 and nominated for a James Beard Award. He practices medicine in Illinois and is passionate about plant-based nutrition and its applications to clinical medicine. He lives in Chicagoland with his wife, Rachel, and three children: Shrey, Radhi, and Reva.